DON LIND
MORMON
ASTRONAUT

DON LIND

MORMON
ASTRONAUT

Kathleen Maughan Lind

Deseret Book

Salt Lake City, Utah

Quotations on pages 102 and 103 are from *Lift-off*
by James C. Hefley. Copyright ©1970, 1972 by
Zondervan Publishing House. Used by permission.

ISBN 0-87579-004-6
Library of Congress Catalog Card Number 85-72357

First printing September 1985

Dr. Robert Goddard, the father of modern rocketry, once said: "It is difficult to say what is impossible, for the dream of yesterday is the hope of today, and the reality of tomorrow." This book is lovingly dedicated to Leslie and Elizabeth Lind, Don's parents, who opened his vision to dreams and instilled faith that makes dreams turn to reality.

Contents

Preface

Feeling very blessed that a man as exciting and dear as Don Lind should invite me to travel the ever-challenging path of life with him, to be his eternal helpmeet, has moved me to say "Thank you" by writing of his adventures so others can also share. This is a gift for Don. I know he would want this written since he has often said so, but he is too busy living these things to put pen to paper, so I have done it for him.

Don gives many talks. We are frequently asked if his talks are in print, with the wish that they were. At first I felt this was the kind of book I should do, to compile his talks given at youth conferences, firesides, and meetings of investigators. But when Eleanor Knowles, editor at Deseret Book, suggested that I write Don's life story, I agreed to try. A feeling of inadequacy enveloped me as soon as I said yes. This sent me to my knees. I said, "Heavenly Father, what have I done agreeing to this? I know _I_ can't do it. But with your help all things are possible. Please help me to remember the stories and events I should include. Please guide me."

It is with humility that I acknowledge the Lord's guidance in this project. Many nights sleep would not come until I got up and wrote things the Spirit was helping me remember. Sometimes I awakened thinking of other happenings long forgotten that should be added. Often as I wrote, the words flowed from my pen as though Don were saying them. In my mind I could hear him telling the stories. For this reason, I have written as

though Don were speaking. He has always said that we fre-
quently think as one and I can read his thoughts. After thirty
years of happy marriage and united goal seeking, we know each
other pretty well. I hope the reader will forgive the license I have
taken in writing this in first person, but in truth we are one.

As soon as a U.S. space program was announced, Don
said, "That's for me!" The thought frightened me a little at
first, but soon it was my desire for him too. When you love
someone, you want that person to reach his goals. His dreams
are your dreams, and your dreams are his.

Don has had the opportunity to do many interesting things
and go to fascinating places. He takes the family when he can.
But when we are unable to be with him, he has a wonderful
ability to make us feel as though we have been there through his
animated descriptions. In this way we have seen many parts of
the world and pierced the heavens with a single-engine high-
performance jet, and now even felt the wonder of weightless-
ness in outer space. Through his eyes, we have gazed from space
at our lovely, fragile earthly home and at other creations of our
Father.

I am deeply moved by a poem entitled "High Flight," by
John Gillespie Magee, Jr., that our former neighbor and good
friend James Irwin has taken as the theme for his High Flight
Foundation:

Oh, I have slipped the surly bonds of earth
    And danced the skies on laughter-silvered wings;
Sunward I've climbed, and joined the tumbling mirth
    Of sun-split clouds—and done a hundred things

You have not dreamed of—wheeled and soared and swung
    High in the sunlit silence. Hov'ring there,
I've chased the shouting wind along, and flung
    My eager craft through footless halls of air.

Up, up the long, delirious, burning blue
    I've topped the windswept heights with easy grace
Where never lark or even eagle flew,

And, while with silent, lifting mind I've trod
The high untrespassed sanctity of space,
    Put out my hand and touched the face of God.

We are moved to say with David the Psalmist: "When I consider thy heavens, the works of thy fingers, the moon and the stars, which thou hast ordained; what is man, that thou art mindful of him, and the son of man that thou visitest him? For thou hast . . . crowned him with glory and honour." (Psalm 8:3-5.)

How grateful we are for the revealed answer: "We have had fathers of our flesh which corrected us, and we gave them reverence: shall we not much rather be in subjection unto the Father of spirits and live?" (Hebrews 12:9.) He is mindful of men because they are his children. He is the literal Father of their spirits.

As children of our Father in heaven, we lived with him in our pre-earthly existence. However, we had progressed as far as we could in that condition. Being a caring and loving parent, he wanted us, his children, to continue to progress until we would become like him and could be crowned with glory and honor.

It is my desire in writing this to let my husband know how much I love and respect him, and to give our seven beloved children a written account of the stories they have heard again and again around the dinner table.

I would like to express many thanks for the invaluable help Colleen Bowman has given in typing this manuscript. Thanks go also to Mark Bowman, Annette Emerson, Lucinda Reeves, and Christine Camp, and to my daughter Kimberly, who helped to edit it. But most of all, my thanks and love to Don. Don has received many honors and titles, but the ones he would rather be known by are husband, father (daddy), son, brother, friend. It is not a profession that makes a man great, but how he treats his family and serves the Lord to build the kingdom of God.

Prologue

As we walked out of the crew quarters, I glanced at the television monitors in our conference room. The space shuttle *Challenger* looked poised and ready. Small vapor plumes indicated that it was fully fueled. Most of the workers had already cleared the launch pad area. The TV camera in the "white room" just outside the entry hatch showed that the technicians were hurrying to be ready for our arrival. From three different angles, on three different monitors, *Challenger* looked impressive and powerful—and beautiful.

Three days earlier, when we had arrived at Cape Canaveral for the last time before lift-off, we had flown our T-38 jets in tight formation over the launch pad before landing at the Shuttle landing strip. The geometry of the launch complex makes a striking picture among the palmettos, sand dunes, and waterways. This morning's trip to the pad was not a flyover nor even a practice run. This time it was the real thing.

Now, just outside the crew quarters, the hallway was full of co-workers, all applauding. If I had thought about it, I'd have known that they would be there. But I had not thought about it among all the morning's details, and their enthusiasm first surprised and then pleased me. Leaving the building, I was ready for the next crowd, which included the network TV cameras. I also saw some personal friends in the crowd and waved. In a brief moment we were seated in the astrovan. Quickly the security escort pulled out and we were on our way. On this trip, unlike all the previous ones, we did not have to stop at any checkpoints. No one would ask to see our badges. Everyone at the Cape knew we were headed for the pad. Back in the conference room, one of the TV monitors showed the progress of our journey.

The van stopped at the base of the gantry atop the launch pad and we walked twenty feet to the elevator. We joked about the implications of the elevator getting stuck, since on our practice run it had gone to the bottom level, back to the top without any command, and returned to the bottom before the door would open. This time it worked properly, and we stepped out at the 195-foot level.

We were almost alone in the usually teeming gantry structure. As we waited to be strapped into our seats, we looked down at the beach and then back to the huge building where *Challenger* had been strapped to its fuel tank and booster rockets. Once we were all settled, it was quiet in the cockpit. Each man's thoughts were his own. As the launch sequence progressed inexorably toward the moment when the engines would be ignited, I was surprised how relaxed I was. When our onboard computer picked up the count at Launch minus thirty-one seconds, I allowed myself a modest measure of emotion. And as the rumble of the main engines began at Launch minus eight seconds, I felt a much larger dose of adrenalin. But when the solid rockets ignited and we surged upward, my emotions gave way to unrestrained elation. It was going to the circus and getting my Ph.D. and celebrating our oldest child's first birthday and going on my first date all rolled into one. We were on our way!

Chapter 1

A Secure and Happy Childhood

When I made my entrance into the world during the great depression of the 1930s, I weighed nine pounds and the nurses called me "the big Swede." But I didn't stay big; in fact, I didn't grow. My parents were worried, though the doctor kept reassuring them, "He is all right, just a slow starter. If he were hungry, he would cry." But I didn't cry and I didn't grow. When I was three months old, my parents took me to a specialist. In a worried tone he told them that I was starving and had not had enough to eat since birth. My resistance had been damaged, and I might not make it. But if they could bring me through five years, I would probably live and be a healthy person.

The formula that I had to eat to build up my resistance cost as much per month as all the other household expenses for the family put together, including housing, food, and transportation. To avoid any illness, I had to be kept away from sick people. Until I was about two, I spent most of my playtime on top of the kitchen table so I wouldn't be in drafts near the floor.

Despite these precautions, I was exposed to some of the children's diseases. I got two types of measles at the same time and my fever soared to 104.8 degrees F. Mother gave me soda baths almost constantly in an effort to break the fever, but I was in a listless stupor for

Elizabeth and Leslie Lind with baby son, Don

several days. I can remember when I finally came to and found myself all covered with spots. I started yelling, "Mama, I've got skeeter bites!"

Because I spent so much time confined to the table-top or my bed, I learned to enjoy mental activities. One time when I was sick, Mother gave me a ball of string and a bottle of buttons to play with. When I wasn't stringing the buttons on twine, I was weaving a string canopy over my bed. I remember winding and unwinding the string over and over again, making different hideaways. Sometimes I would pretend to be a bear hiding in my string cave. Other times it would be a tent, or a fort to protect me from Indians and wild animals. I couldn't play the rough and tumble games that other children did, for fear I'd become ill, so my parents read to me often and emphasized learning and self-discipline. To build my strength, I was taught to know and live by the Lord's law for good health, the Word of Wisdom. I am certain that without this close adherence to its teachings, I would never have been able later to pass the unbelievably strenuous physical I was given to enter the astronaut program.

My father aroused my interest in physics before I even went to school. I can remember as a tiny child asking him why the moon looked the way it did, why it eclipsed, and what eclipses were. Dad would take me into the bedroom and turn out the lights. Then, using a flashlight, he would be the sun; Mother would represent the earth with a beachball, and I would be the moon with a tennis ball. Under his tutelage, I learned about the phases of the moon, levers and wedges, inclined planes, and other fascinating principles of physics. I could do problems in long division before I entered first grade, because my parents took time to explain things to me.

I conducted my first experiment in physics when I was about three. We had a large home with a closed-in back porch. The porch was a great place for a little boy to ride his tricycle, except that it had a long stairwell— seven steps leading from the back porch to the back door, and another seven steps going from the door into the basement. My father, being a prudent man, put a gate at the top of the stairs, but it wasn't long before I could get that open. It was great fun to pedal up to the edge of the top step and then back away. Pretty soon I found I could actually let the front wheel go down over the edge a little and then backpedal hard to bring it up to safety again. At some point I realized that the wheel would slip and I wouldn't be able to back it up. But I was determined to see at what point this would happen. What I didn't realize was that I wouldn't discover that point until I had just exceeded it. Mother found me head over heels, two-and-a-half somersaults later, and dizzy as a dervish at the bottom of the steps.

Though I gave my parents a scare, the experience only whetted my appetite to be a scientist. Through the years I have suggested in many talks to youth audiences

Leslie Lind with son Don in
wheelbarrow

Don Lind in front of childhood
home

that sometimes young people (occasionally older ones too) get caught up in a similar type of experimenting. As unmarried couples, they try to see how involved emotionally they can become in kissing and necking and still "pedal back." They don't realize, as I didn't with my tricycle, that there is a point at which you get out of control and cannot turn back. So if you don't want to go all the way with the two-and-half somersaults, I tell them, don't ride tricycles at the top of the stairs.

When I was two and a half, my sister Charlene was born. They say I chose her name. I had been listening to a radio program called *Baron Münchhausen* when Daddy came to tell me I had a new little sister. All through the program the Baron kept saying, "Vas you dere, Charlie?" So when Daddy asked, "What shall we name our baby?" I replied, "Charlie." The closest girl's name my parents could find to Charlie was Charlene. We still sometimes called her Charlie as a nickname. When my parents brought my new little sister home, I took my favorite blanket, smoothed it out over her, and put her finger in her mouth and my finger in mine to show her how to suck it. "This is how you do it," I said.

Charlene and I have been good friends ever since, except for the time when we were young and she chased me around wielding a knife because I had stolen some of the batter from a cake she was making! It's a good thing I am a faster runner or I might have lost something important. Cake batter, particularly chocolate, is one of my weaknesses. I'd rather have this than the baked cake anyday. When I was a teenager Mother taught me to make cakes. For quite a while my contribution to the Sunday meal was always a cake for dessert.

By the time I started grade school, my health was much improved. As I grew stronger and able to play outdoors, Charlene and our cousins Mont and Barbara Deming and I would spend many hours in the gully just across the corral. We lived great adventures there. Our favorite was to take space trips in our "rocketship" tree.

My sister Kathleen, whom we call Kathy to avoid confusion with my wife, was born when I was thirteen. It was fun having another baby in the family, but when I was left to tend her, she would howl from the time our parents left until they returned. When they went out, they would go to elaborate lengths to sneak away without her knowing. My father would carefully let the car coast down the driveway past her bedroom window so she couldn't hear the engine. But somehow she would still know, and she'd start to cry as soon as the car left the yard. I'd walk the floor with her for hours.

Superman and He-Man are heroes of many children today, but when I was young, my father was superman to me. As a little boy I knew he was very clever and understood all kinds of machinery; I was also sure he was one of the strongest men in the world. That gave me a tremendous sense of security as well as an example to follow.

We lived in the home my mother had lived in as a girl

*Don and Charlene Lind
proudly hold baby sister,
Kathleen*

in Midvale, Utah, just south of Salt Lake City. The huge
barn made a great place for a little boy to play. Then my
father decided to tear down the barn and replace it with
a smaller one for our one cow. The original had been
built by a man who obviously thought it needed to last a
thousand years. Dad decided to cut out sections of the
walls for the smaller structure. I was amazed that he
planned to let the sections fall to the ground without re-
straint. I thought they would be broken to pieces, but he
said the air pressure would cushion their fall, since the
air had to be forced from under them just before the impact. Sure enough, he was right. I was very impressed
that he knew exactly how it would all happen. I was
even more impressed that he was able to singlehandedly
lift the wall sections into position for the new barn. He
had an ingenious array of levers and props, but I knew
that most of the force was Dad's immense strength.

Most of my youth Dad worked in refrigeration. He
installed most of the big refrigeration units in Safeway
stores in the West. I think he could fix just about anything. After I got married, whenever my folks came to
visit us they would say something like, "If you want us

to visit and just talk, we will be glad to, but we will stay only a few days. If you want us to stay longer, then make us a list of things we can fix for you. We aren't content unless we are busy. When we run out of things to do, we will go home." They upholstered our furniture more than once, and always fixed everything in sight that needed repairs.

My parents' home was at the top of a hill on a lane a mile from the center of town. A canal ran beside our lane. When I was in junior high school and was taking a woodworking class, I decided to make a canoe. It was a bigger project than the teacher had assigned, but I was determined. The canoe turned out quite well, and my friends and I had lots of fun floating it down the canal. In winter, ponds in the meadows below our house froze, making a wonderland where we could skate and slide.

We didn't have a lot of money, but our parents felt this should not keep us from seeing and enjoying the world we lived in. Every year we would go on a family vacation. Sometimes we went to Bryce, Zion, Grand Canyon, or Yellowstone national parks. We loved to camp and hike. Often we would camp for a week at a time at the Spruces in nearby Big Cottonwood Canyon. Vacations were joyful experiences. Though we never had a really good car, Daddy could always fix whatever broke.

Our parents instilled in us a feeling that we were capable of doing anything we set our minds to do. And they were always there to cheer us on. I was an enthusiastic Boy Scout partly because my father was an enthusiastic Scout leader. I went on to get my Eagle, and Dad would have gotten his too if age limits hadn't been adopted at that time. He had filled the requirements. My wife, Kathleen, comes from a scouting family too—her father was an Eagle and also received the Silver Beaver. Our son David is also an Eagle. So we have three generations of Eagle Scouts in the family.

Mother and my sisters were very active in 4-H clubs,

Mother as a leader and the girls as members. They all became expert seamstresses. One year Mother took first
place at the Utah State Fair with a winter coat she had
made, while Charlene and Kathy won ribbons and
awards at county and state fairs year after year. In truth,
the whole family got involved in 4-H. Every summer the
4-H groups would go camping in the Wasatch Mountains. Dad always helped set up and take down the
camp, but since he had to return to the valley to work
during the week, I became camp helper and general
gofer.

I was never a 4-H member myself, but the year I was
a senior in high school, I was recruited to shepherd a
group of ten- and eleven-year-old boys whose leader
could not go. Mother had agreed to take them with her
girls' club if I would go along to help. As soon as we set
up camp, I realized that I had a real challenge on my
hands—how to control a dozen or so boys with un-
bounded energy. I decided I would have to drain off
some of their energy.

My first opportunity came when the entire camp
hiked to a lake in the mountains. At the first rest, the
boys and I took off ahead of the girls. I set a good steady
pace for myself, and since the boys' legs were much
shorter than my own, I really pushed them. We arrived
at Dog Lake long before the rest of the group. By the time
the girls arrived, we were soaked to the skin from playing on floating logs in the lake. I insisted that we wait
until everyone else had started back down, and then we
took off our wet clothes, laid them on rocks to dry, and
went swimming.

When we were ready to start back to camp it was almost time for lunch, so I set a blistering pace down the
mountain. By the time we got to camp, I was leading
some very tired boys. After lunch I sent the boys off to
do handicrafts while I had a long nap in my hammock.
The handicraft leaders reported that my boys were little

Don as a teenager

angels. I knew they were too tired to have caused any mischief.

The next day all of the activities took place in camp, so I didn't have an opportunity to wear them down. But that evening, I told the boys the most hair-raising, heart-chilling stories I could make up. By the time I finished, every forest voice was full of evil portent. Then I went to my hammock and slept soundly. Two of the boys claimed they sat up back to back and never shut their eyes all night. The next day the boys were all so tired that they weren't any trouble at all. My system for keeping them worn-out worked marvelously.

That evening I had the most embarrassing experience of my youth. Since I was not a 4-H'er myself, I elected not to go to the campfire program. I stayed in camp to get things organized for our return home the next day. Since the camp was deserted, I was wearing only the briefs that I slept in. I had intended to be in the hammock in my sleeping bag when everyone returned. However, as I was getting a drink of water, I heard voices and realized the campfire program was

over. Flashlights were coming down the trail just beyond my hammock. Since some of the girls were my
own age, I didn't want to be seen in my scanty attire,
so I sprinted across the camp, jumped onto the hammock, and tried to get into the sleeping bag. But I didn't
pay sufficient attention to my balance. The hammock
flipped over and dropped me about five feet onto my
back on the gnarled elbow of a root. I groaned with pain,
unable to breathe. Just a few feet away, a girl's voice
shouted, "There's something in the bushes! Maybe it's a
wild animal!" Suddenly, several flashlights were aimed
at me, and another voice screamed, "It's a naked man!" I
was humiliated. I can't ever remember being so embarrassed. As soon as I could catch my breath, I crawled
deeper and deeper into the bushes. Finally the flashlights moved on down the trail, and I crawled into the
hammock. The "naked man-creature" was never iden-
tified, and most of the camp leaders attributed the problem to the imagination of some excitable girls. However,
my teenage psyche was scarred for life!

Education always received high priority in our
home. While my father was on his mission, Mother
taught school. At home, emphasis was placed on pursu-
ing learning all of our life. With this kind of example, it
was not too surprising that I should start my Ph.D. program in graduate school even though I had three children, and didn't complete my program until we had five
children. My sister Charlene went on to get her Ph.D.
and is an associate professor in the Clothing and Textiles
Department at Brigham Young University. My sister
Kathy got a degree in clothing and textiles and is an ad-
ministrative official at the University of Utah.

No one said to me when I was young, "Don, when
you grow up, why don't you be an astronaut?" Outside
of the funny papers, there were no astronauts. When
young people ask me today what they can do to start
training for an astronaut career, there is nothing really

The Lind family: mother Elizabeth, Charlene, father Leslie, Kathleen, Don

specific I can tell them. By the time they get to the point of making application, the entire space program could have changed and the requirements could be different from the ones I had to meet. I can give them advice, though. It is important advice, not only for an astronaut but for any goal they wish to achieve. The advice is this: *Always do your very best.*

You may think this is a trite statement. Many young people do not realize how significant it is until too late. But doing or not doing your best has underlying effects that can make or break the attainment of your goal.

Let me tell you my own experience. When I was being considered for the astronaut program, I had to be cleared for top-secret work. The FBI checked me out thoroughly. They talked to many people who had known me: friends, neighbors (a neighbor woman was even asked if I had made passes at her!), relatives, teachers, and employers. The investigation was so thorough that some people asked my parents whether I was in some kind of trouble because the FBI had been asking about me. Suppose I had not always been quite honest. Then at some stage of the screening, if a neighbor or an acquaintance had said, "Yes, I remember that Lind boy, he used to steal hubcaps," that would have been the end. And it would have been no use my protesting that I had done it only for fun.

Now does the advice to always do your best seem trite? Hubcaps may not appear to be significant enough to mention, but even a misdemeanor like that does count in the final analysis. Everything we do in this life counts, because each action adds up to or subtracts from the total person and his strength.

This is where Latter-day Saint youths have such an advantage over any other group of young people in the world. They have the training and the goals before them early in life. These goals are right and worth following. Any young person who dedicates himself to the teachings of the Church and adheres to its principles will never have to be embarrassed or make excuses when someone starts checking out his life. I do not say that everyone should blindly follow along in the Church. I do say that everyone must gain a testimony of the gospel for himself in order to have something on which to anchor.

Chapter 2

How My Testimony Developed

Many years ago the great pioneer leader Heber C. Kimball said: "To meet the difficulties that are coming, it will be necessary for you to have a knowledge of the truth of the work for yourselves. . . . If you do not, you will not stand. The time will come when no man nor woman will be able to endure on borrowed light. Each will have to be guided by the light within himself."

My evaluation process began late in high school or early in college, when I enrolled at the University of Utah. I am not in the least embarrassed that I reevaluated my testimony. I think that a testimony of the gospel is something that everyone at some time in his life has to look at very closely. I didn't want to believe the gospel just because my mother and father said it was true and because they didn't lie about other things. I wanted to know for myself whether the gospel was true. I needed my own light. I didn't set out to challenge Mormonism, but rather to discover its truth for myself. I am still continuing that quest for evidence, as my testimony grows stronger and stronger.

Many little things assemble themselves together to make up the greater whole of truth. Whether Joseph Smith was a prophet of the Lord seems to be one of the things every convert has to grapple with. One point has impressed me concerning the Prophet. Joseph reported

that Moses had visited him and given authority for the
Jews to return to Palestine, their promised land. The
Jews had been claiming for many years that they were
about to go back to the Promised Land. Even to this day,
every time they celebrate the Seder supper at the Pass-
over, they pray, "Tonight we eat the supper in Bremer-
haven (or wherever they happen to be), but *next* year in
Jerusalem." They had said this for two thousand years,
and yet almost none of them went to Jerusalem until
Joseph Smith, under the authority received from Moses,
sent Orson Hyde to dedicate that land for the return of
the Jews. This he did without television cameras, without the press corps, and without telling the Jews. But
after two thousand years, something inspired this branch
of the house of Israel to go home. They started gradually, but by the late 1940s they were willing to buck
the entire British navy, which had formed a blockade
around unpartitioned Israel. Every Jew that the British
caught was sent to detention camps in Cyprus instead of
to Jerusalem, but the people were willing to take that
risk. I think the Lord was inspiring those Jewish people
because of the action taken by the Prophet. I was an
Aaronic Priesthood youth when the Jews were strug-
gling to get back, and I remember reading about it and
being thrilled that I was seeing a prophecy fulfilled.

Such kinds of evidence were a tremendous tes-
timony-builder to me as I came to know of them, and I
am glad I have had the opportunity to study and learn
and continue adding to my testimony.

Another awareness that grew as I studied is that
there are a lot fewer potential conflicts between LDS
theology and science than between general Christianity
and science. Most of the modern Christian faiths have
the concept of a God who is large enough to fill the universe and yet small enough to dwell in a person's heart.
This idea is very difficult to square with science. It just
doesn't make sense. It is not even good logic—to have
something, yet nothing. Karl Marx said that religion is

the "opiate of the masses," meaning that it is more or less useful only to keep people in line so they can be controlled. A lot of people who certainly wouldn't consider themselves to be communists and would probably be offended if they were so accused seem to go along with the idea that religion is just a very pleasant collection of fairy tales and legends and should not be taken seriously by people of learning. Of course, I do not agree with this. I have known a few people who have turned away from religion because they felt it was intellectually unacceptable to claim to have a testimony.

I saw an example of this attitude when I was working toward my Ph.D. in physics at the Lawrence Radiation Laboratory at the University of California. I was working with some extremely brilliant young scientists. One day we learned that the parents of one of the students were members of the Christian Science faith and that he had attended this church as a child. This young man was embarrassed when we heard this, because he found the religion of his parents intellectually incompatible with the profession in which he was trying to educate himself. I don't think any Mormon need find the teachings of The Church of Jesus Christ of Latter-day Saints intellectually embarrassing.

Some people have suggested that science and religion are basically different, that they involve themselves in different questions (which is probably true), and that they are incompatible intellectually. I challenge the incompatibility part of that statement. Science and religion use different kinds of tools, but I think they are intellectually compatible, since a person who is well-educated can also have a testimony. He need not be ashamed of his testimony and he need not compromise his intellectual standards when he considers the gospel. As a youth striving to get my own testimony and also as an aspiring scientist, I was overjoyed to find how comfortably they fit together.

The first challenge that is thrown up to any church

(and I am defending only ours, because I think ours is in a far superior position) is that science deals only with tangible quantities. We can always measure them on scales, or read them on ammeters, or count them electronically. Or we can test our specimens in wind tunnels, or grow them in a laboratory, or observe them with a microscope or telescope. The challenge is that religion is less reliable because it often deals with intangibles such as faith and revelation. But I don't think this distinction is really accurate.

I wrote my dissertation at the University of California at Berkeley on pion-nucleon interactions. I have never seen a pion and I have never seen a nucleon, and yet I published an article in *Physical Review* (which is the "doctrine and covenants" of physics), and I expect the scientific community to take that article seriously. But I never touched anything I worked with. It wasn't tangible; I couldn't get hold of it.

In sophomore physics, we learn about inductance or magnetic field lines or capacitance. Has anyone seen or felt inductance or a magnetic field or capacitance? We can measure only their effects. And when we read about quantum mechanics, it may seem that the scientific community has completely lost touch with reality; there is nothing tangible. We can't even visualize the elements of quantum mechanics. They are just smudges of probability. So I suggest that scientists sometimes deal with the intangible and that they do this with *no* intellectual embarrassment.

We are told that science is superior to religion because in science, we can experiment to learn its data. Every sophomore has the scientific method explained to him until he can practically repeat it in his sleep. The essence of this explanation is to forget one's prejudices and make decisions only in terms of the available data. That is the scientific method.

If that is science and experimentation, the gospel is

susceptible to the scientific method. The Lord gives us several examples. For example, concerning tithing, he said: "Bring ye all the tithes into the storehouse, . . . and prove me now herewith . . . if I will not open you the windows of heaven, and pour you out a blessing, that there shall not be room enough to receive it." (Malachi 3:10.) That is just an experiment. Many people have testified that they've tried the experiment and it works. That is the process of science. It is not an intellectually different kind of a thing.

Alma says, "Experiment upon my words." (Alma 32:27.) He then goes on to compare faith to a seed that, if we will water and feed and nurture it, will let us know whether the message is good.

The Savior gave us another example. He said that if we want to know whether the doctrine is true and comes from the Father, we must "do his will." Then we "shall know of the doctrine, whether it be of God, or whether I speak of myself." (John 7:17.) This is all that science asks us to do—simply judge on the basis of the data.

We are also told that while science deals with experiment, religion deals with faith—and faith is supposed to be an intellectual process unknown to the scientist. This is obviously not true. Galileo (1564–1642), the great Italian astronomer and physicist who is often called the founder of experimental science, is a good example of a scientist who had faith. He invented telescopes that could see farther than had been seen before. His first important observations in astronomy concerned the moon. He discovered that the moon was not a smooth sphere shining by its own light; rather, its surface was marked with mountains and valleys, and its light was only reflected light. Galileo agreed with the theory of Copernicus that the earth moves around the sun, rather than the earth being the center of the universe with everything turning around it. These observations did not agree with the teachings of Aristotle and of the Catholic

Church, so Galileo was dragged before the Inquisition, forced to endure a long trial, and punished. But he never lost faith in his finding. I believe that his confident belief in the things he had discovered was the same mental process in religion we would call faith. He stood by his beliefs even when he was treated cruelly.

Science and religion do not employ different kinds of mental processes; rather, they share a great many things in common. And I suggest that The Church of Jesus Christ of Latter-day Saints and the gospel principles that it teaches are susceptible to scientific analysis. I believe that we can analyze the gospel, ask questions about it, and look into its challenges scientifically.

Before we do that, we have to look at the kinds of questions that we can ask, because if we don't ask the right kinds of questions, we can't get intelligent answers. There are basically three kinds of questions we can ask. The first kind is *question of fact*. These are to be answered simply by looking at the real world. How high is Mount Everest? That's a question of fact. We can measure it. The answer to such a question may not be readily available, but it is still a question of fact. A question of fact has nothing to do with how many people know the answer, or accept the answer, and it has nothing to do with public opinion or with so-called "authorities." If it is a question of fact, it can be answered simply and solely by observing the real world.

Next, there are *questions of logic*. These do not deal with the real world, but rather with some system of logic that we have defined: therefore, these questions are simply to be checked against that logical system. If A is greater than B and B is greater than C, then it follows that A is greater than C. If we make the syllogism, "All Scotsmen have red beards, and John is a Scotsman," then it follows that John has a red beard, regardless of what real Scotsmen and real people named John are like. These are questions of logic. They have answers, but they are to be judged only by the system of logic that we have defined.

Finally, there are *questions of value.* Almost every question of value has a word like *good* or *right* or *better* in it. We might ask a question such as, "Is Beethoven's music better than Wagner's?" That is a value judgment, and I suggest that it has no real answer. If we ask if it is louder or more contrapuntal, those are questions of fact, and we can find out the answers. But "Is it better?" is a question of value. Generally such questions have no demonstrable answers because we have no standard by which we can determine the correct answer.

Now, if we ask the wrong kinds of questions, or if we don't realize whether we are asking questions of fact or of value or of logic, we won't get intelligent answers. For example, if we ask, "How many coins do you have in your pocket?" this is a question of fact. But if we assume it is a question of logic, we might approach it this way: All persons who drive cars must take into account parking meters. Therefore, you, being an intelligent person, will carry at least a few coins in your pocket for parking meters. This may or may not be logical, but it has nothing to do with the facts. Nor is it a value question, such as, "Is it *right* for you to have some money in your pocket (because I don't have any in mine)?" We simply ask you to empty your pockets and we count the coins; that is all there is to it. It is a simple question of fact, and we can't arrive at a reasonable answer if we approach it any other way.

In the Church, most of the basic questions we ask are questions of fact. Did Joseph Smith see God the Father and His Son Jesus Christ in the Sacred Grove or did he not? This question boils down to just as much a historical fact as who won the Battle of Hastings, or how high is the highest mountain on the back side of the moon. These are questions of fact, and they do not depend on value judgment, emotion, or exercises in logic.

People have said, "It's not logical for God the Father to have appeared to an obscure country lad in New York. If he had appeared to the Pope or the Archbishop of Canterbury, he would have started off with a million members and would have converted the world by now." That may be logical, but it has nothing to do with the facts.

Or they may say it is not right, for some reason or other, for God the Father to have appeared to Joseph Smith. That has nothing to do with the facts. Either God the Father did or he did not appear to Joseph Smith. Either there is a God, or God is dead. These are all questions of fact. Is there a God? Was Jesus Christ divine, or was he just a very nice person, a good teacher? Did the Father and the Son appear to Joseph Smith? Is the recipe for salvation as described by Joseph Smith the one the Lord set up, or did he set up a different one? These must be investigated as questions of fact and not questions of either logic or value.

What is the primary reason that members of the Church become inactive? I suggest it is not because of the doctrines but because of people. They lose their faith in people. They don't like the way the bishop did something; a quorum adviser was unkind to them; or they don't like the way the Primary teacher treated their little boy. This has the same kind of logic as saying, "I don't believe the world is round any more, because Columbus offended me." And to say "I don't believe that Joseph Smith saw God because I don't like the bishop" doesn't impress me as being scientifically sound either.

How, then, do we get a testimony of the gospel, or how do we keep it? I suggest that since I was not in the Sacred Grove with the Prophet Joseph Smith, I have to judge whether or not he saw God on the basis of *secondary evidence*.

I wrote my dissertation on pions without ever seeing any pions. I don't know whether they are green or

round or square or fuzzy, but when we turned on the
cyclotron beam in the meson cave (a room made out of
twelve-foot-thick lead-impregnated concrete blocks),
the beam struck a hydrogen target and splattered particles in all directions. Certain detectors that I had designed and had placed in appropriate spots in the cave
registered these particles by sending out electrical im-
pulses. All that I actually observed was a series of two-
volt jumps in the voltage on some coaxial cables. By
fitting the pattern of these blips together, I published
what I claim is a scientifically accurate explanation of certain pion-nucleon interactions.

This is scientifically sound, though it is all based on
secondary evidence. No scientist has ever been inside a
nuclear fireball voluntarily, yet one can tell you microsecond by microsecond what happens inside a nuclear
fireball, or inside the sun, planets, or stars. No elec-
tronics technician has ever been inside of a vacuum tube,
to my knowledge, and yet one can tell you for an entire
semester what goes on inside there, based entirely on
secondary evidence from detectors. In the same way we
can find out what went on in the Sacred Grove through
the secondary evidence of prayer, faith, study, and good
works. I was not in the Sacred Grove in the spring of
1820, but I think I know what happened. I have faith that
Joseph Smith told the truth.

The Book of Mormon is another statement of fact.
Some of the points that stand out in Dr. Hugh Nibley's
writings have impressed me as evidence on whether or
not Joseph Smith wrote the Book of Mormon. He either
forged it and had to guess at thousands of details of an
unknown culture, in order to get every detail correct, or
he got it from an ancient source that was written by an
eyewitness.

To borrow from Dr. Nibley, if every compound (and
there are many) of the name Ammon, a Book of Mormon
name, follows the correct rules of Egyptian grammar,

and if the verse in which Lehi admonishes Laman to be
like a river continually flowing into the fountain of all
righteousness is in the authentic format of the oldest
form of Arabic poetry, and if Joseph Smith knew all
this, he obviously had an amazingly good education in
the Vermont and New York school systems prior to the
1820s. The fact is, though, that Egyptian grammar and
Arabic poetry were not taught in Vermont and New
York schools in those days, and not in any colleges
either. This is modern scholarship. The first work on
ancient Egyptian grammar was done by A. H. Gardiner
in 1929, a hundred years too late to have given Joseph
Smith any help. Thus, it is easier for me as a scientist to
believe that Joseph Smith had an ancient document from
which he translated the Book of Mormon than it is to believe that he correctly guessed the correct compound
name form under the rules of Egyptian grammar and the
proper Arabic poetry form and a myriad of other little
details. It is easier for me as a scientist to believe this than
that he could possibly have forged such a volume. I have
more faith in the power of God than in the power of
man. These evidences, coupled with the witness of the
Holy Ghost, have made it possible for this scientist to
have a testimony as to the veracity of the Book of Mormon.

   One thing that has helped me to keep apparent conflicts in perspective is simply to remember what the Lord
has told us and what he has not. As a youngster, I used
to worry about where the ten lost tribes were. I stopped
worrying when I read a remark Elder James E. Talmage
made when he was a mission president in England. "If
I knew where the ten lost tribes are," he said, "they
would be the ten *found* tribes." The Lord has told us
that they have been hidden from man, and that should
suffice. We don't need to worry about their whereabouts.
We are told they will return and come from the north.
How they will return and when is really the Lord's con-

cern, and I've found it easy to have faith to leave it like that.

There is some argument over evolution, the Bible versus the biologists. Genesis, the Book of Moses, and the Book of Abraham tell us that God created the world, that he had a purpose in doing it, and that man is very important in that purpose. These books are not intended as a handbook on how God created the worlds. They just say that he did it. Someday he will let us know how he did it. Science is theorizing on the how, but there need be no conflict when we remember what the Lord has told us and what he hasn't.

I have sufficient faith that in due time the Lord will fulfill all the prophecies and predictions he has made and that these things will come about just as he has told us they will. Actually, if we have eyes to see, we have seen many of these fulfillments taking place in our day.

When I was a child, in my family we would put together a huge jigsaw puzzle each Christmas, one that would take a week to finish, with thousands of small, look-alike pieces. I hated to do the sky. It was very difficult to put together an all-blue sky. But my mother liked that part of the puzzle, and she usually chose to start working on one of the upper corners of blue sky. It would have been foolish to argue with her that her piece of blue sky really belonged down in my blue water, because neither of us could be sure about it at that point. But what we did know was that each piece fit in only one place, and that we could complete the picture only by placing each piece correctly. When the Lord allows the scientists to discover all their part, and he sees fit to reveal his part, it will be the same completed picture.

This is how I have come to look at the plan of the Lord. We need to stop worrying about each small piece and try to fit the whole picture together by keeping in mind the end result. The Lord knows where each piece goes and how it fits into his plan. Each of us should help by putting ourself, an intricate and important piece of that puzzle, in the proper place.

That is one reason why a mission is important. On a mission you can really start putting the pieces together. It is wonderful to be able to bring meaning to other people's lives, as you can on a mission, and let them see where they fit into the Lord's plan. I have always appreciated the fact that I went into the mission field with a testimony. It was greatly strengthened while I was there, but I went out having one because of my earlier seeking through study and prayer, when I decided as a youth I needed to know for myself, not just rely on my parents' testimonies.

Chapter 3

Missionary Service
in New England

At the end of my sophomore year at the University of Utah, I received a call to serve a mission in New England. I had always known I would go on a mission; after all, hadn't we talked of it since I was tiny? Hadn't Dad left five days after his wedding to serve thirty months as a missionary in the Hawaiian Islands while Mother taught school to support him, setting the family example? And hadn't Mother been saving pennies all my life for this purpose? All through my formative years, she took the pennies left over after every shopping trip and handed them to me to put in my little missionary bank. When the bank was filled, we would take it to the big bank to add to my mission account. This was done again and again. Hadn't I always dreamed of going? Yet when the time came, there were dissenting voices trying to dissuade me.

I had been a debater in high school. Now I was again doing it in college. My partner and I had advanced to national ranking. Our debate coach had visions of a national championship, and we had a good chance. We had almost gone to the national finals as sophomores, which was almost unheard of. We missed going by one vote in only one decision during the West Coast finals. Both we and our coach felt confident that with two more years, our junior and senior years, we had a good chance to take first place in the nationals. But if I went on a mission, my partner would have graduated by the time I returned.

In the end there was really no decision to make, however; the decision had been made many years before. I debated for the university again when I returned, and I received individual national honors, but as part of a team I never made it to the national championship. However, I have never regretted my choice. In the eternal scheme of things, the mission was where I needed to be right then.

In 1949 the New England Mission was presided over by Elder S. Dilworth Young of the First Council of the Seventy. It was an honor to have a General Authority as our president. The mission consisted of the six New England states (Massachusetts, Connecticut, Rhode Island, Vermont, New Hampshire, and Maine) and the Maritime Provinces of Canada (New Brunswick, Nova Scotia, Prince Edward Island, and Newfoundland). This is a big area. When I was working in Newfoundland I was nearer to the mission office in London, England, than to my own in Cambridge, Massachusetts.

When we arrived in Boston, President Young said, "Some of you elders are probably disappointed that you weren't called to a foreign-speaking mission. Let me tell you that you were. Several foreign languages are spoken within this mission. The people who speak them think they are speaking English, but to you they will sound like foreign languages." I soon found what he meant. It was not just the dialect, but words I thought I knew had different meanings. One time we asked an old gentleman if he could direct us to a certain place. "Ay-ya," he said. We gathered this meant yes. "I'd goo oot thay-er 'bout two sees," was his answer. This meant, Walk as far as you can see and then walk as far as you can see again.

As it turned out, I had to learn to recognize (if not to speak) several "foreign languages," since each area had its own dialect. I served in Vermont, Nova Scotia, Newfoundland, and Massachusetts. I had the privilege of baptizing the second and third members of the Church in Newfoundland. To join the Church there at that time took great faith and courage, because it meant being ostracized from almost everything. The state church, which was Pentecostal, owned and operated all schools and cemeteries in the province, and many other things too. If a person left the state church, he ran the risk of not having a school for his children or even a place to be buried. I remember dear Sister Mercer telling me that she was willing to sacrifice all these things because she knew The Church of Jesus Christ of Latter-day Saints was true, and she had faith the Lord would provide. She felt a need to have her friends see the truth of the gospel. She said, "Elder Lind, the true church should make us better people if we live what it teaches. If I am not a better person after joining the Mormon Church than I was before, my friends will say that I had no business being baptized. They need to see a change for the good in me. But, Elder Lind, this is hard because I was trying to be as good as I thought I could be before, when I was a Pentecostal."

I served as president of the Newfoundland District. As part of my responsibility, each month I filled out a financial report. Since there were not many members, our funds never exceeded one hundred dollars, so there wasn't much to report. At the bottom of the report was a space for remarks. I didn't know what to put there, so to pad out the report I would write in the current mission jokes. About ten years later I was on Temple Square in Salt Lake City one day when Charles Schmidt, one of the auditors for the Church, rushed up to me and said, "I have wanted to talk to you for a long time, Don. I audited your reports from the Newfoundland District a few years ago, and they were the most interesting things I have ever audited. Usually that stuff is pretty dull." I hadn't realized these reports would go beyond the New England Mission headquarters.

In Vermont I tracted without purse or scrip. It was a very humbling experience, but one I am grateful for. My companion and I would store all of our belongings except what we could put in one half of a small suitcase; then we filled the other half with copies of the Book of Mormon. From spring to late fall we had to rely on the Lord and the generosity of the people for bed and food.

The Lord provided for us well. Usually we would only have breakfast and supper. We would tell the people how we were traveling, and they would offer us a place to stay and a bite to eat. At noon, instead of eating, we would have study class by a stream and wash our clothes. We even gained weight on this fare. Only once did we have to sleep in a school (very uncomfortable) and once in a barn whose hayloft was more comfortable than most motels. I soon wore out my shoes walking from village to village.

The work went slowly with few conversions. It had been over one hundred years since Wilford Woodruff had been able to convert whole villages in New England and on Fox Island. We wrote regularly to the mission president and told him of our activities. One day, with little new to add since the last letter, my companion wrote in discouragement, "Dear President Young, My companion and I, after talking it over, have decided that most of the blood of Israel in Vermont joined the Church and went to Nauvoo, and then moved west with the pioneers. We think that today the blood of Israel that is left here is shared roughly equally between the missionaries and the mosquitos." Whenever President Young saw Elder Woodfield after this, he always asked him how the blood of Israel was doing.

Apparently not all of the Israelites had gone west, though, because a few very choice Saints were gathered in during this time. Brother Morris Laroux, who owned a large dairy farm, was baptized in Burlington, Vermont, the same day I arrived there to start my mission. About three months later, President Young came to Burlington for a branch conference. Brother Laroux asked for a few minutes to talk to him. He told him that he wanted to pay his tithing. He had calculated all the money he had earned in his lifetime (he was then in his thirties) and estimated that his current assets were probably about equal to one-tenth of his to-date lifetime earnings. He said that if he sold his dairy farm he could pay his tithing, but if he did so, he would be broke. Would the Church consider letting him pay it off a little at a time instead of all at once? Then he could keep his farm and continue to earn a living, and in the end the Church would receive more in tithing. President Young was flabbergasted. After a moment he said, "Brother, didn't the missionaries tell you that you are only asked to start paying tithing from the time you joined the Lord's church?" "Oh, President Young, that's easy!" the convert exclaimed.

One marvelous older sister I knew in Vermont was in her eighties when she met the missionaries and gratefully accepted their message. All her life she had been a pillar of the Methodist Church in her little village, always holding several jobs. When she accepted the gospel and joined the Church, she felt an obligation to her former church to explain her action, so she went to the minister and told him she was grateful for all he had taught her. But, she said, she felt like someone who had always been taught that high school was as far as you could go in education and then had discovered that there was college beyond that. She said she would never walk away from the truths she had learned in her former church, but she was now able to add to it. What joy her knowledge-hungry soul had received when she found that the Lord had a "college" where she could learn more of heavenly things.

President J. Howard Maughan   *Sister Hattie B. Maughan*

I had been on my mission almost a year when a new mission president was appointed, J. Howard Maughan from Logan, Utah. The Church did not at that time have a teaching plan for the missionaries. We just said what was in our hearts. An organized plan of teaching had been written and tried in another mission. The wife of one of our missionaries, who had been serving in the mission where the plan was used, came to meet her husband on his release and brought with her this new plan. President Maughan was excited about the new program and anxious to get it out to the missionaries. The former missionary sister agreed to stay a while and train a few key missionaries who would then teach the others how to use it.

I was one of the elders President Maughan felt inspired to call into the mission home to prepare to teach the others. However, I was working in the country and he didn't have an address or phone number where I could be reached. After several fruitless inquiries, President Maughan went into his office, knelt down, and prayed. He told the Lord he felt the new missionary plan would advance the work, and that one of the elders he needed couldn't be located by human means. Would He please find the elder and inspire him to call the mission home? Before many hours I felt impressed by the Lord to report into the mission home. I hunted up a phone and called President Maughan. He told me, "I knew it wouldn't be long till you would call. I have a special assignment for you. Bring your things and come right into the mission office." This triangle of communication through heavenly powerlines truly endeared President Maughan and me to each other.

One day I commented to Sister Maughan that someday I wanted to have a happy marriage like hers and President Maughan's and like that of my parents. I asked if she had any suggestions on how to choose a companion. "I'll tell you what Elder Adam S. Bennion told us when I was in his seminary class," she said. "He told the boys they should look around for some great parents. 'Find a woman you can really admire,' he said, 'and then marry any of her daughters who will have you. Apples usually don't fall very far from the tree. The daughters would likely grow to be like their mother.'" (I'm sure the same advice goes for girls; they should find a father with the admirable traits they want in a husband and then hope he has a son.) Well, I didn't have to look far to find the parents I admired. They were right there, presiding over my mission. Too bad their only unmarried daughter was Kathleen, a teasy, flirty scamp.

The eight missionaries in the mission office lived in the mission home with President Maughan's family. One day Kathleen helped fix breakfast by laying a sheet of clean gauze on the waffle batter as it cooked; when the waffle was done, the gauze didn't show at all. I was served this piece. I kept cutting and cutting the waffle but couldn't cut a piece off. I didn't know what was the matter, but a couple of people were trying to stifle giggles. Another time, on April Fool's Day, while her parents were attending general conference in Salt Lake City (Sister Gale, the cook, was chaperoning), Kathleen set off the mission home fire alarm at 2:00 A.M., sending the mission staff leaping out of bed.

Later on when I became a counselor in the mission presidency (now they are called assistants to the president), we had a meeting at which President Maughan talked about a problem in the mission. We were far from Church headquarters, and there weren't many members, especially eligible young LDS men for the girls to date and marry. However, there were all these handsome elders just the right age. The mothers kept inviting the missionaries over to dinner and to do their washing, and the daughters were always flirting with them. President Maughan said, "We have to recognize the mothers' problem. They want their daughters to marry Church members, which is the right thing. We need to sympathize, but then fight against them." After a pause he added, "But I guess I need to set my own house in order first, don't I." After that, for a while in our inner circle Kathleen was referred to as "My House." Little did I know then that the fates intended me to one day set up housekeeping with "My House." We were married on April 1, 1955, in the Salt Lake Temple—the nicest April Fool's joke ever played. Would anyone be surprised to note that we took as our family theme the resolve of the prophet Joshua, "As for me and *my house*, we will serve the Lord"?

This was three years after we had met. In that time Kathleen had also filled a mission. I'm glad we didn't fall in love while we were in the mission field. It would have taken our thoughts away from the important work we were doing. But I am glad we built a foundation of friendship and shared experiences there. Marriage is so much sweeter if, besides loving each other, you are also best friends.

Chapter 4

Flight Training in the U.S. Navy

The Korean conflict was going on when I returned from my mission. I would have been inducted into the infantry immediately if my father, in his wisdom, had not already registered me for some classes in college. If you were a registered student, you were deferred. He had signed me up for classes without my knowledge, but I was grateful. I was able to continue through to graduation, getting one deferment after another. By pushing, I was able to do the undergraduate work in three years—two years before my mission and one after.

As a graduate, I was eligible to apply for Officers Candidate School (OCS). I can see as I look back that the Lord has guided my steps to lead me to where I am now. If Dad had not registered me for school before I returned from my mission, I would have been a private in the army. If I had not gone into the service as an officer, I would not have been permitted to become a flyer, which later led to my becoming an astronaut. When I was young, there was no such thing as a space program. I really didn't know I was preparing for this, but I tried to do my best at whatever I did; then I let the Lord take the lead, to guide me to where I am.

After OCS I went to Pensacola, Florida, for primary flight training. I arrived on a Saturday night. First thing the next morning, I found the address of the Church in

the phone book. I figured meetings would begin about
nine o'clock, so I arrived at 8:30. A brother greeted me
with a warm handshake. When I told him my name, he
said, "Oh, you're the new elders quorum teacher." I
said, "No, you have the wrong person. I just arrived last
night. This is my first time here." "You are Don Lind,
who just finished OCS in Portsmouth, Rhode Island,
aren't you? And you were the branch president there?"
"Yes." "Well, then you're the one!" It seems my reputa-
tion had preceded me, and I had already been called to a
job.

Soon, besides learning to fly propeller airplanes, I
was on the district council of the mission, traveling regularly to visit branches in northern Florida and Alabama.
This was a happy fate for a hungry bachelor, because
the sisters always put on a marvelous potluck dinner
between the conference sessions, each sister trying to
outdo the others with her edible fare.

Kathleen and I were to be married at general conference time in April, when her parents would be permitted to leave the mission for a few days. With luck, I
would just be finishing up my primary flight training
and would have a few days of leave to transfer to Corpus
Christi, Texas, for jet flight school. As the time approached, I found I was about ten days ahead of schedule in my training. President and Sister Maughan would
still be in New England when I would have to report in
Texas for advanced training. Our trips to Utah would
not coincide. And what about the reception and the
announcements already sent out? Panic set in. What
should I do? I went to my trainer, told him the problem,
and asked if I could slow things down a bit. He said,
"Have you ever been susceptible to colds?" That was it!
If I was stuffed up, I couldn't fly. The altitude pressure
would force fluids into the eustachian tubes, causing
pain that might be dangerous.

Since Pensacola is located on the Gulf of Mexico, I

went down to the beach and scooped up a small bottle of saltwater. Then I went back to the bachelor officers' quarters and started doctoring myself with an eyedropper of saltwater in each nostril. Soon the back of my throat felt stingy and my nose was stuffy. I went to the flight surgeon and told him I had postnasal drip and felt a bit stuffed up. He looked in my mouth and nose, and said, "Yes, you seem to have a cold. We'd better ground you for a day or two." He gave me some medicine, which I took home and put on the shelf. But each day I would faithfully take my saltwater nose drops. The trip to the doctor was repeated several times, always complete with medicine and repeated advice to remain grounded. By now I had quite a line-up of medicine on my shelf. When I thought the training schedule would work out right, I quit taking my "medicine" and recovered. It was good to start flying again.

A further extension of this story: I had recently purchased my first car, a Studebaker. One day I went out in my swimming trunks to wash and polish it, and a cold wind came up. Horror of horrors, I got a real cold—and now I was in danger of not finishing on time! I poured the medicine the doctor had previously given down me in as large doses as I could, and with sheer dumb luck I was finally able to finish on time.

Jubilantly I started driving to Utah, a graduate of primary flight training, in my brand new car, about to take a bride. The world was mine! But either Satan was trying to stop me from taking an important eternal step or the Lord thought I was being too cocky and could use some humility, because while I was going through a small town in Louisiana, a speeding car whipped around a corner and used my car as a ricochet. The entire left side of my car was caved in eight inches. Miraculously I wasn't even injured, but my pride and joy looked less than lovely. It could be entered only from the righthand side. The other car didn't even stop, and since this was the middle of the night, I couldn't find a policeman, so I just continued on, shaken but very thankful to be alive. I arrived home safely and was happy to discover that it was really me, not the car, that Kathleen wanted to see anyway. We were married as scheduled in the Salt Lake Temple, and after the reception, we honeymooned en route to our new assignment in Corpus Christi, Texas.

One of my goals at that time was to go to graduate school and get my Ph.D. in physics. I felt that my time in the service was a detour from that goal. But since I had to be there, I decided I might as well enjoy the time by doing something interesting—like learning to fly. Here again, the Lord was guiding my way. I was signed up for a four-year tour of duty. We decided that while I was in the Navy, we could save the money we would need for graduate school if we spent only the basic pay I received and saved all flight pay.

We were certainly grateful later that we had done this and had a nest egg put away. Later, when we started graduate school at the University of California at Berkeley, we found it would cost more to rent an apartment than to buy a house and make house payments. With the money saved while in the service, we had enough for a down payment. At that time the house cost only $13,000, and we paid $65.00 each month on the mortgage. After graduation we sold the home for $16,500. This was like having free rent all the time we were in graduate school. Now we had a bigger nestegg for a down payment to put on the next house. Each home we have had has been bigger and better than the last one, because back in our military days we saved half of our money even if it meant missing out on some of the extras many of our friends were enjoying.

Our first home was on the Navy air base in Corpus Christi. The base movie theater was a short half-mile away. It cost only ten cents per person. I had learned a bit of useful information while reading about airplane

*Don and Kathleen Lind,
newlyweds*

"thunderstorm penetration procedures." You should try to avoid thunderstorms if you can, but if you can't, then be prepared ahead of time. Lightning is common in thunderstorms, and one flash of lightning can wipe out the night adaptation in your eyes. But if you shut one eye, you will be all right. If a lightning flash goes off, switch to the eye that has been closed, and you can still see. Shut the other eye and hope it will be night-adapted by the time another lightning flash goes off and you have to switch again. I discovered this was a great tool when going to the movies. We would walk over to the theater in bright sunlight, and I'd wear my sunglasses so no one could see that I had one eye closed. Most people, when going into a darkened theater, have to wait until their eyes become adapted to the dark before they can find a place to sit, or else stumble down the aisle, feeling around for a seat. Not me! I could walk right in and immediately find a seat because I had one eye night-adapted. It was my wife who would stumble over people, wondering how it was that I could see where I

*Don and Kathleen just after
she pinned his Navy wings on
him*

was going. She laughed when I told her what I was
doing, but I noticed it wasn't too long before she too
could walk right to a seat in a darkened theater.

When we got married, Kathleen had one more quarter of college to complete before graduation. She was
majoring in elementary education and had already done
her student teaching. She took several correspondence
classes while I did my jet flight training, but to graduate,
she had to be on campus, so she went back to BYU for
the last half of summer school. By then she was pregnant with our first child. Most of her classes were early
in the morning, just when she was feeling the worst
with morning sickness. She missed enough classes that
if she hadn't had an understanding professor, she
would not have made it through and graduated. Bless
Brother James Clark!

Soon after she returned, I finished jet flight school
and was promoted to lieutenant. Kathleen pinned on
my Navy wings. I was assigned to a flight squadron at
Miramar Naval Air Station in San Diego, California, so
we packed up our car and headed for the West Coast.

I had been teaching Kathleen to drive with a standard shift. She had just gotten over the "jackrabbit" routine, where she would stall every time she stopped at a stop sign or military base gate, roar the engine to get going again, leap forward, then stall again. On our move to the West Coast, I let her practice driving on the long, empty stretches. One thing still bothered her, though, and that was to pass a car or, worse still, several cars or a truck going the same way we were. If she started gaining on a vehicle far off in the distance, she would begin to worry and wish that it would turn off the road before she got to it—and invariably it did. This went on for about a hundred miles or so. Every time we would begin to overtake another vehicle, it would stop or turn onto another road. I began to think this little wife of mine had powers I didn't know about!

Our baby was due soon after our one-year anniversary in April, so in late January we enrolled in a "getting ready for your baby's birth" class. There was a series of lessons, but we could enter the class at any point. It turned out that the first lesson we went to was on labor. We were starting at the end of the series! However, this was fortuitous because that very night the baby decided to come, two and a half months early. Because of the lecture and movie we had just attended, we recognized what was happening and got Kathleen to the hospital in time.

Before we left for the hospital, I gave Kathleen a priesthood blessing. I felt impressed to tell her that both she and our little one would be all right. This comforted us both. Although our tiny baby girl weighed only two pounds eight ounces and had to stay in the hospital in an incubator for two months before we could bring her home, we had the comforting assurance from the Lord that our little Carol Ann would make it.

Our second child, David, was also born in San Diego while I was in the Navy. He made an entrance as dra-

matic as Carol Ann's. Both baby Carol and Kathleen
had contracted whooping cough and were ill for several
months. Since Kathleen was pregnant, the strenuous
coughing caused this baby also to come early. He was
born at seven and a half months and weighed four
pounds fifteen ounces. When labor started, I took Kathleen to Coronado Island Naval Hospital. There we were
told that their only isolation ward for communicable diseases was for men. Since she had whooping cough, she
would have to be taken back to the San Diego County
Hospital to give birth. The baby was getting closer to
arrival, so I insisted that Kathleen be taken in an ambulance with a nurse present. I drove our car in close formation behind them. Though a long line of cars was
waiting for the Coronado ferryboat, the ambulance
driver could see he needed to be in a hurry, so he com-
mandeered the ferry. Only the ambulance and our car
got aboard. Then, with siren howling all the way, we
wove in and out of traffic and just barely made it to the
hospital in time. David was born a few minutes later in
the admittance room of the County Hospital isolation
ward.

Though David was a preemie, he had to be put in the
pediatric ward because he had not been born in a sani-
tary deliver room. He got infectious diarrhea there and
started going downhill. When Kathleen was able to go
home, we had David moved to the Navy hospital. The
doctors there couldn't stop his diarrhea and vomiting,
and after two weeks they said, "We've done all we know
how to do for him. Maybe his parents' love will do something we can't. You'd better take him home." Kathleen's
mother came and spent some time helping take care of
things, and when she went home, my mother came.
Kathleen was still in a great deal of pain because all the
coughing while pregnant had expanded her rib cage,
and then when the baby was born the rib cage snapped
back together, pinching a nerve. The pain lasted for sev-

eral weeks until the nerve finally died. We browned and boiled barley, then gave David the watery juice from this to drink, and his problems were eventually brought under control.

Before we got married, Kathleen and I had been working on the requirements to become a Golden Gleaner and Master M-Man. We decided to make this one of our first goals together. Some of the requirements we had filled had not been signed off, and the whereabouts of some of the people needed for signatures was a problem. Finally my paper came back with the last signature on it. However, Kathleen's paper didn't return. We sent many letters trying to track it down. She had worked almost five years to fill the requirements, and now the paper that recorded all her achievements was lost. The time limit was running out, since the paperwork had to be completed by a certain age. We both felt disappointed, because an important goal to both of us looked impossible to reach. I would receive my award, but it didn't have the luster it once had. We prayed that somehow this important paper would be found.

That same day, as Kathleen sat outside the bishop's office in the foyer of the ward, she overheard the bishop say, "I surely wish I knew who this belongs to. A lot of work has gone into it. I've had it on my desk for some time and don't know what to do with it. I hate to throw it out, but I don't know what else to do. I can't imagine why it was sent to me in the first place. We don't have a Kathleen Maughan in our ward." At this, Kathleen jumped to her feet, grateful the door had been ajar and that she had overheard the bishop. Apparently she hadn't changed her name on the paper to Lind when we married, thinking the people who had to sign it would not know her by her married name. She rushed in and said, "Bishop, that's me! That's my maiden name." The long-awaited paper had been on his desk for a month and was on its way to the "circular file" when the Lord answered our prayer. Never would we doubt that he is a loving, caring Father, concerned about the little things that matter to his children. He tells us he will help us reach our righteous goals, and I know that is true.

As part of my Navy training our squadron spent several months practicing aerial gunnery over the Southern California desert near El Centro. We were flying FJ-3M Furies, at that time the Navy's best day fighters. It was a one-man plane that generally flew at 650 miles per hour. We flew four planes in tight formation, which meant each plane was only two feet away from the next plane's wing tips. The pilot of the lead plane had to be the eyes for everyone, watching for other planes. Each of the other three must keep close track of the plane beside him to avoid a midair collision. Another Fury pulled the banner we were to practice our gunnery on. We usually flew in formation but would separate to make individual gunnery runs, then rendezvous to fly in formation back to the base.

The banner was made of a very heavy fabric. Each plane carried colored tracer bullets that would leave a mark on the banner if they hit it. This way the officials could tell which pilot had been accurate in his firing. The banner was attached to the tow plane by a 1,200-foot metal cable that was strong enough to take a direct hit with a 20-mm cannon shell without breaking. The tow plane was slower than our planes because of the drag of the long, heavy cable and banner. The tow plane was always supposed to have an escort plane flying with it for safety.

One day only two planes were in our flight formation, and the escort plane for the tow was out of his proper position. I was flying the second plane, in the rear of the formation. The lead plane had sighted the escort and started flying in that direction, supposing the banner for our gunnery run would be there. Since the escort plane was out of position, the lead plane didn't realize how close he was getting to the tow plane and banner. He and I saw the cable at the same time just as we were practically on it. He yanked his plane up to go over, while I dived down to go under—and didn't quite make it. If I had followed the lead plane upward, the cable would have hit me squarely. As it was, it ticked the windscreen in front of me and glass shattered, covering me with bits of broken glass. Fortunately my head was protected by the helmet and oxygen mask. I went into a nose dive, wondering if the rest of the windscreen would break, and if it did, would my shoulder straps hold me in?

The cable had severed, so the banner was floating to the ground. When the pilot in the tow plane reported over the radio, "I think someone hit the cable," frantic voices began asking if I was flyable and what my condition was. But I was too busy trying to find that out myself. I was in a nose dive and about to go supersonic. Only one man at that time had ejected supersonic and lived—and I didn't propose to be the second, because he had been seriously injured. Just in time I pulled out of the dive and found I was flyable, and only then did I report over the radio that I was OK. I made it to a safe landing, filled out an accident report, and went home.

Before we were married, I had written to tell Kathleen that I had signed up for flight training, and this had concerned her. She later wrote that the night she received my letter, she had talked to God about her concerns, telling him, "Father, Don wants to become a Navy combat pilot. You know me—I'm an old worrywart, and I'm going to worry about him because I love him. But I'll make myself sick if I worry constantly. Please help me not to worry when I don't need to. When he is safe, please help me to feel that he is safe and not to worry unduly. Speak peace to my heart." All through my flying career she has felt at peace with a very few exceptions—and this was one of those exceptions.

When I arrived home that evening she was pacing up and down, knowing something had gone wrong. It wasn't just that I was a little late and we had a date; she had really felt uneasy all day. Since we were in a hurry, I felt that the accident needed more time to explain than we had, so I didn't tell her what had happened. I planned to tell her later. When she asked, "Is something the matter?" I reassured her, "Everything is okay."

We had been to a number of squadron parties, but this one was different. It was a gathering of the entire Air Group Command. We had no sooner walked through the door than the group commander came over and said, "Mrs. Lind, may I have this dance?"

As they danced away from me, I could guess what they were talking about. The first thing he said to her was, "Kathleen, we sure are glad to have your husband here tonight." She thought, *Aren't you glad I'm here too?* but said, "Oh, we wouldn't want to be any other place." He went on, "Well, if your husband was not a good Mormon, he wouldn't be here. The good Lord saved his life this afternoon!" The look on her face told him I hadn't said anything about the incident to her. She asked, "What do you mean? I don't know what you're talking about." Then he told her of the accident. "It was not Don's fault," he reassured her. "But we are lucky he wasn't killed. There is a small strip of metal on the windscreen. The cable must have hit exactly on that and been deflected. If it had hit a fraction of an inch lower or above, it would have cut right through the windscreen and probably decapitated your husband. Yes, I'm a Catholic, but I think the good Lord liked the Mormons today."

Missions came in many forms. I found a second mission in the Navy. One of two things can happen in the service: you can stand on your own two feet and keep your sense of values, or you can drift with the world. Military life can be a great character builder if you make

Don with his parents just before he went overseas with U.S. Navy

it so. I had some choice spiritual experiences there. But there was also much temptation, if I had chosen to give in to it. Some in my flight squadron set a goal when we went overseas to get me drunk and into a brothel. I made sure I never went on liberty with any of them. I went around with the Latter-day Saint enlisted men though I was an officer, and this association was frowned upon by others.

On the aircraft carrier USS *Hancock*, I was the only officer who was a Mormon and the only returned missionary aboard. I served as the assistant group leader. Once when we were in the center of Tokyo Bay, we ordained a young man to the office of a teacher in the Aaronic Priesthood.

We had a missionary plan of our own devising. Some of the Latter-day Saint sailors were great at asking the golden questions. They could sometimes reach people when no one else could. They would ask the questions, get an interest worked up, and then bring the contact to me for some teaching.

One young man we taught was a plane captain. This

meant he had to physically be in or around his plane as long as the aircraft was on deck. He was responsible for seeing that it was fueled, oiled, and clean. During flight operations he would sometimes be attached to the plane from before dawn until after dark. It was difficult to hold cottage meetings under such circumstances. But we found a way. I would sit on the wing of his aircraft on the carrier deck in the middle of the Pacific Ocean and hold a cottage meeting with him. It was a delightful experience teaching the gospel with the ocean thundering around us and flying fish arching beneath the bow.

All the discussions for the missionary plan were given to him in this manner. By the time we reached Hong Kong, he was ready for baptism. After he had been interviewed by the mission president in Hong Kong, I had the privilege of baptizing him in the swimming pool at the mission home in Kowloon. I have maintained contact with this fine young man since that time—I was the best man at his wedding, for example—and it thrills me to know that today he is still very active in the Church.

Aboard the *Hancock* we had an LDS meeting every single day, not just on Sunday. If a meeting was not scheduled, we would organize a study class. Such military experiences can be just as faith-promoting as corresponding experiences in the mission field. They are truly uplifting. They make the spirit soar.

Our squadron head, Commander Vince Kelley, was a truly fine man, but while we were on cruise he had an ulcer, and the longer we were at sea, the more surly he got. He had one great passion, a hatred for the New York Yankees baseball team. He avidly followed their games, venting his venom each time they won, which they were doing often that season. His disdain was general for the whole team, but with special vehemence for Whitey Ford and Casey Stengal, who could do nothing right. Some of this sourness splashed over onto the men of the squadron.

Shortly before the ship was to arrive in Hong Kong, I started growing a mustache, which was allowed by the Navy at that time. When Commander Kelley saw it, he yelled, "What's that growth on your upper lip?!" And he ordered me to shave it off. I didn't want to shave off the mustache and didn't think the commander had the right to order me to do so. However, I was afraid he might not let me go ashore in Hong Kong if I didn't, and this was where we were hoping to baptize the plane captain whom we had been teaching. So I shaved the mustache off. But it rankled a bit, so I decided to do a favor for Commander Kelley in return.

In secret, I wrote to Casey Stengal and Whitey Ford and told them that our commanding officer followed their team very closely—which he really did. I said it would greatly impress him (I didn't say make him happy) to get a personally autographed picture. Whitey Ford didn't reply, but Casey Stengal sent back a large photograph of himself with the inscription "To my good friend, Vince Kelley, from your pal Casey Stengal" written across it.

When he opened the package, Commander Kelley almost came unglued. At first he was livid; then he exploded. But gradually he began to think it was funny. He began interrogating all the officers in the squadron to find out who had played this trick on him. He knew that none of the enlisted men would have dared do it. When he came to me, he said, "Lind, did you do this?" I didn't deny it; rather I said, "Now, Commander Kelley, what on earth would make you think I would have a part in it?" "Because you are enjoying it the most," he said. Then he went on to ask someone else.

When my tour of duty ended and Commander Kelley signed my release papers, I told him I had been the one who had written to Casey Stengal. He said, "Don, you can't know how much that meant to me! It's very lonely at the top. You don't feel a part of what the rest of the squadron is doing and you're rarely included. But this once I was in on the joke. I was the center of it. Thanks. I appreciate it more than you know." And we parted friends.

My four-year tour with the Navy was completed. The next day I flew from Japan back to the United States and to my dear little family in Utah, where they had been staying with Kathleen's parents. We had been apart a long seven months.

Chapter 5

Graduate School
and a Growing Family

After my release from the Navy, we stayed in Salt Lake City for a year. I taught a few physics labs at the University of Utah and also took some extra physics classes to get me back into the educational swing for graduate school. The next year the University of California at Berkeley accepted me as a graduate student with an appointment to do research work at the Lawrence Radiation Laboratory.

We were about to have another addition to the family. Since the first two children had come prematurely and Kathleen had been having a few problems carrying this one, we didn't want to risk another early birth, so when I went to California, Kathleen and the little ones stayed in Utah with her folks to have the baby there.

Dawna arrived at the dawn of a lovely early fall day. As the streaks of pink lighted the sky, Kathleen told her mother, "Don would rather not have a junior. He feels that everyone should have his or her own name. But if this is a girl, I'd like to name her after her daddy but spell it like the dawn of the morning." When she was young, this dear little girl took delight in surprising her mother by doing things to help around the house without being asked.

As our family grew (we had five children by the time I earned my Ph.D.), we found it harder to get by on only the small pay from the fellowship. I needed another job. We both agreed we wanted Kathleen to stay with our children. Thanks again to my Navy training, I was able to get a job flying as a "weekend warrior" with the Naval Reserve. I did this only one weekend each month, but it paid as much as I would have received had I pumped gas for a few hours every day.

While flying with the Naval Reserve, I had an experience that taught me a lesson. I had been on a cross-country flight, and when I returned to Alameda, my home base, I found they were having a big, very formal inspection. The only outfit I had to change into was my khaki uniform, but everyone else was in formal whites. I felt extremely uncomfortable and out of place. I could hardly wait to hide. It felt terrible being different from everyone else. I imagine this is how a person would feel if he could somehow climb under the fence into the celestial kingdom but didn't really deserve to be there. It is very uncomfortable being out of place. Probably those in the telestial kingdom wouldn't really be happy if they could get to the celestial kingdom.

We enjoyed going on temple trips to the Los Angeles Temple. We would board the chartered bus in the evening and, by traveling all night, arrive at about five o'clock in the morning, just in time for the first session. We'd go to three sessions and then turn around and drive back home. We always commented that surely the celestial kingdom must be like this, associating with people of such spiritual strength. We felt a loving one-ness with all these good people.

The day the Church announced that a temple would be built in Oakland was a joyous day, but we wondered where we would get extra money so we could contribute to the building fund. Just at that time the Naval Reserve announced that one could get extra flight pay by flying on Thursdays also. The Lord may not have inspired this just for our benefit, but it certainly came at the right time. I went to see my graduate adviser, Dr. Bert Moyer. I told him of my special need for money to help with our church building fund. Then I explained that I flew with the Naval Reserve and had the opportunity to do some extra flying, which would provide the money I needed. The problem was that the flying would have to be done on Thursdays. I asked him if it would be possible for me to work at the Radiation Laboratory twice a month on Saturday instead of Thursday. He agreed, then said, "I am a lay minister in my church, and it's very hard to get people to contribute. Are all Mormons as anxious to contribute as you?" I told him I hoped they were.

On days when I drove the car to school, I sometimes went over to the Oakland Temple site to see how the construction was progressing. Since it was the noon hour and the workmen were eating, I'd walk all through the building, certain that they wouldn't throw me out. I went so often that one day the supervisor came over to me and asked, "Who are you—an inspector for the construction company or the city?" I said, "Neither. I'm part owner." This only made him look perplexed.

While I attended graduate school in Berkeley, we lived in Concord, California. I bought our home while Kathleen remained in Utah to have the baby. I drove away from Berkeley until I found housing we could afford. This meant a commute of about twenty-five miles each way. To get to the university, I had to go through a tunnel through a mountain. Most of the six years we were there, either the road or the tunnel was under construction or repair, resulting in long delays. I felt I was wasting a lot of time in commuting. This made me determine that when I got a permanent job after graduation, I would buy a house as close to the front gate as possible. This is why my office at the Johnson Space Center is only about a half mile from my home near Houston.

One time as our family came out of the tunnel on our way home from Berkeley, we heard a loud bang and felt the car wobble as a tire blew out. This occurred only about fifty yards beyond the tunnel entrance. We felt the Lord had been looking after us. Had this happened while we were still in the tunnel, it would have been impossible to pull off to the side and avoid an accident.

Fortunately others in Concord were going to U.C.– Berkeley, so I was able to join a car pool. At first I felt a little distressed when I learned that we had to leave home an hour early just so one of the men could buy breakfast when he got there. Then I discovered this was just the time I needed to do my scripture reading. With the intense pressure of graduate school, I found that this early-morning scripture study, a noon class at the LDS Institute of Religion, and my nighttime retreat to the peace of home were the only things that kept me going sanely clear through to my Ph.D.

Two more children were born to us while I was in graduate school. The first was Douglas. When he was born, I was working around the clock on an experiment that was run on the cyclotron. A friend had to take Kathleen to the hospital, but I got there before the baby arrived. I don't know how we could have ever made it without helpful friends during those years. While Kathleen and the baby were in the hospital, the children needed to be tended because I had to be at the lab. Thoughtful friends were right there to help. Carol, David, and Dawna had a gift for their little brother when Kathleen brought him home. They had all come down with mumps. We felt grateful Douglas was too little to accept this particular gift; he apparently still had immunity from his mother so he didn't catch it.

When Doug was still just a baby, Kathleen dislocated her shoulder in an accident. She was returning from Primary with a car full of children. Douglas was in a car seat next to her, and three-year-old Dawna was by the right front door. Dawna knew she should have her seat belt on, so she tugged and pulled, but it wouldn't come

Carol Ann, Dawna, and David Lind

loose. Then she discovered the reason: it was caught in the door. Well, she knew the only way to get it loose was to open the door (the car was going 50 mph). Kathleen saw what was happening and was able to reach over Douglas to yank the door shut before Dawna tumbled out. But in doing so, she dislocated her shoulder. It was extremely painful. She was in the fast lane of traffic, next to a cement abutment, with no place to pull off and in so much pain that she could not control the car. She looked in the rearview mirror quickly and saw that no cars were behind her for some distance, so she put on the brakes and stopped. There she sat, in the fast lane of traffic, with cars swerving around her, a car full of children, and her arm painfully out of joint. She moaned, "Oh, what am I going to do? My arm is out of joint. It hurts so bad, I can't drive the car!" Six-year-old Carol said, "Mommy, you always tell us we should pray when we have a problem." So Kathleen asked Carol to pray. As the short but earnest prayer ended, the shoulder slipped back into place. Kathleen had dislocated her shoulder before, but never had it slipped back in so easily. It was always a very slow, painful process.

We felt that the Lord had helped her this time, but that the problem was no longer just a nuisance—it could endanger the family. For this reason, we decided Kathleen had to have an operation to correct the problem. With the mother in our family out of commission for several months and me busy night and day at the university and the lab, our parents once again came to the rescue. Carol and David went to stay with Grandma and Grandpa Maughan in Logan while Dawna and Douglas stayed with their Lind grandparents in Salt Lake City. A special, loving relationship grew up between the children and the grandparents they stayed with. After twenty years Doug still remembers the bow and arrow and quiver Grandpa Lind made for him, and David happily recalls fishing trips with Grandpa Maughan.

The rest did Kathleen good, but we both missed our children terribly. By the time we were able to go to Utah to bring them back home, baby Doug was not sure he wanted to go to these parents who had deserted him, but he got over this quickly. Kathleen flew to Utah first, and I drove to get them a little while later. The Maughans brought Carol and David from Logan to the Salt Lake airport when Kathleen arrived. My parents also brought Douglas and Dawna. When three-year-old Dawna started running toward Kathleen with arms out, Kathleen's heart started to pound. She had missed her babies so much! But Dawna ran right past her and into the arms of her sister Carol, who was behind Kathleen. The whole family had been missing each other.

Kimberly was born as I neared the completion of my work for the Ph.D. Graduate school had been a difficult period of our lives. For years we had been pinching pennies, and I had been too busy at work and school to be a lot of help at home. With four children under seven

Don Lind when he completed graduate school: front, Douglas, Dawna, baby Kimberly; back, Kathleen, David, Carol Ann, Don

years of age, Kathleen had had her hands full. But now we were seeing the light at the end of the tunnel— graduation was in sight. After that there would be a regular job with more pay and, we hoped, fewer hours away from home and family. I felt that the whole family was getting that degree, not just me. Kathleen and the children had sacrificed with me, and now this sweet baby girl, our fifth child, had come to bless us. Kimmy seemed like my graduation present. Kathleen and I felt greatly loved of the Lord that he would share all of these choice children with us.

When my work at the lab was finally completed, my dissertation signed by the last professor, and the house sold, we headed for Washington, D.C., where I had a job at the NASA Goddard Space Flight Center. Two years later we moved to Houston, Texas, where I would begin training as an astronaut.

Three weeks after we arrived in Texas, our precious baby Kimmy, now just turned three, was hit by a car at the beach in Galveston. She had been playing with other little ones in water only a few inches deep. Suddenly she jumped up, scrambled out of the water, and ran into the path of the car. At that time cars were allowed on the beach. The car wasn't going very fast, but the bumper hit Kimmy over the left ear, knocking her down. The car passed over her, but the wheels didn't touch her. However, her skull had a very bad fracture. A friend who was with us carried consecrated oil in his car, so we gave her a blessing as she lay sobbing on the sand. As I laid my hands on her and pronounced the blessing, she immediately stopped crying. My first thought was *She is dying*. But then I felt the Spirit of the Lord and knew she was going to make it. What a humble feeling it is to realize you might lose one of your dear ones, but that you can call upon the power from God to hold the child here and help her to get well.

Kim had to be hospitalized for about two weeks. Because of the blow to her head, she forgot how to do some things. It was a thrill to see her relearn to talk and walk. When she came home from the hospital and our family was reunited (the other children had been cared for by loving friends), the feeling in our home was beautiful. Realizing we had come close to losing one of the family members made us all feel more loving and protective of each other. We knew that if she had had to leave us and we were obliged to "lay up a treasure in heaven," we would someday be reunited because of our eternal family relationship. But we gratefully thanked the Lord that he had let her stay.

Chapter 6

Acceptance into the Space Program

When I was little, I used to play with some friends in an old elm tree and pretend that this was our spaceship. It was built into our imaginations by Buck Rogers, a twenty-fifth century comic-strip character with whom my generation grew up. We would simulate the whoosh of motors and the sound of miles slipping past our silver rocketship by shaking the branches of the trees and letting the leaves rustle against each other. Those were my dreams long before our scientists envisioned manning the moon. They were dreams that hung in the closet of my soul for many, many years. When the announcement came that the nation was really looking for spacemen, those memories urged their way out of the closet.

The Eisenhower Administration announced the start of the space program, and when the Kennedy Administration said there would be a manned space program, I told my wife I was going to apply. She said they would obviously not consider married men, which seemed reasonable; so, being five children beyond bachelorhood, I decided to forget the whole thing. To my surprise, when the original seven astronauts were named it turned out they were all married men.

Astronauts are recruited in groups. In the first and second groups, only test pilots were allowed to apply.

In the third group, nontest pilots could apply. I could hardly wait to submit an application.

Of course, there were formal requirements to be met: you couldn't just send in an application like a cereal-box top and get your space badge. I had met all of the formal requirements except the one that called for a thousand jet flight hours. I had flown jet aircraft in the Navy, including flying from aircraft carriers, and had logged a total of 850 hours, 150 less than the stipulated 1,000. On the other hand, while the requirements called for a bachelor's degree, I had a Ph.D. I argued with myself that the Ph.D. was worth the 150 deficit jet flying hours, so I applied to NASA.

I was unsuccessful. I had not met the formal requirements set forth, and with that I was rejected. I appealed and asked for a waiver of the requirement I had not met. Again I was refused.

I couldn't believe they really meant no, so I got a plane from the Naval Reserve and flew to Houston to see whomever I could see. Once there I found out that they really did mean no. It was tempting to see whether they would consider accepting 150 hours spent in an elm tree, but I didn't ask. I returned home, striving to maintain some hope in my heart that I might get another crack at the job. This hope gradually declined, and after about a year I resigned myself to a life other than that of an astronaut.

Announcement of the fourth group came shortly after I had decided to quit trying. The announcement brought me fresh hope: they were recruiting scientist-astronauts! My Ph.D. was in high-energy nuclear physics, so the scientist requirement gave me no problem. I had made up the 150 hours of jet flying time in the Naval Reserve. A close look established that I now met all the formal requirements but one: I was now 76 days too old! For the first time there was an age limit. Even with the help of the elm tree, the Naval Reserve, and the Ph.D., there was no possible way I would be able to fulfill that requirement.

I managed to solidify a good argument in my defense. I knew how to fly a jet, so I could save about nine and a half months of training as compared with scientists who had no flight training and had to learn how (the first thing this group did after their selection as astronauts was to go to flight school). Again I made application, but because of the 76 days, I was turned down. Again I applied for a waiver. Again I got the thumbs-down treatment.

But somehow I couldn't give up hope, and trying, and preparing. During the next year I faithfully continued calisthenics and jogging. I had laid out a two-mile course that I would run nightly. I follow the biblical admonition to "go the second mile," but it says nothing about the third or fourth. Neil Armstrong said to me at the astronaut gym one day, "When we were born we were given only so many heartbeats for our life, and I'm not going to waste a one on jogging." I decided early that I wouldn't run marathons, but maybe I ought to go the second mile. This was before jogging became the rage, and I was somewhat of an oddity. I wore a canary yellow jogging suit on my 11:00 P.M. runs. I picked up many dogs who would run along with me, and once in a while a policeman would cruise along beside me, wondering what robbery I was running away from. One night as I came near a house, I heard two women laughing their heads off about something. As I passed, one pointed and said, "Oh, there he goes now!" Apparently I was the village idiot. I have sometimes wished I could go back and tell them what I was doing and that it paid off.

After I completed my Ph.D., I had applied for a position with NASA doing space physics at the Goddard Space Flight Center. Working for NASA, I was at least closer to the program, if that was any consolation. While I was waiting for the next group announcement, if there

Doug Lind

*Jogging was part of Don's
physical training for astronaut
program, a regimen he
continues to follow*

should be one, I designed an electronic spectrometer
to look at the electrons in the solar wind, which is part
of the interplanetary medium. This device flew on the
OGO 5, the Orbital Geophysical Observatory number 5,
an unmanned spacecraft.

At last, requirements were announced for candidates for the fifth group of astronauts, and this time I
met them all, including age. (There was an age requirement for only the fourth group.) I felt sure the officials
had finally written a set of requirements just for me.

During my years of watching other groups pass me
by, I had written, called, and pleaded with nearly everyone in the NASA program. By then I was on a first-name
basis with many of the top people at Houston. I immediately phoned Houston and asked for Jack Carroll,
personnel manager. His secretary said, "Oh yes, Dr.
Lind from Goddard. We were wondering how soon you
would call." My comment to Jack Carroll was, "Okay,
Jack, take my folder out of the drawer and put it in the

stack on the table." NASA had all my specifics, since I had been hounding them for so long.

By no means did this telephone call get me accepted. There was a rigorous physical examination to pass, followed by the selection board interview. But it wouldn't surprise me if I learned that Jack Carroll had walked into the office of Deke Slayton, the man who would give me the initial checking-out, and said, "Look, just bring him down and give him a physical to get him off my back." Anyway, Mr. Slayton called and asked me to come down to Houston. At last I was on my way to getting somewhere—or at least I hoped so.

In aspiring to be part of the fifth group of astronauts, I would be competing with some of the best pilots in the United States, particularly some excellent test pilots. The selection committee was composed entirely of test pilots. I had to prove that I was not senile and that I could meet the physical competition on which test pilots pride themselves. As I entered the Brooks Air Medical Center for my physical exam, I knew I not only had to do well, I had to surpass my competition. Was I glad I had kept myself on a rigid physical-fitness program all those years!

The physical exam took six working days. That gave them enough time to give us every test we could think of and a few of which we had never heard. We thought some might have come from the Inquisition.

The first battery of tests was related to the heart. This was designed to make sure we could stand the stress tests later. The heart test was a tiger. There were vector cardiograms, electro-cardiograms, and anything and everything else to do with the heart. I passed those tests all right and went on to the stress tests.

One of the most critical stamina tests, and one at which I felt I had to particularly shine, was the treadmill. This was simply a belt that moved too fast for a walk and not fast enough for a good, comfortable jog. When the test begins, the treadmill is level. Each minute it raises 1 percent, so at the end of twenty minutes the person being tested is going up a 20 percent slope (which is an extremely steep slope), and he must still travel at the same rate of speed. During this test, instruments record every beat of his heart and his pulse and breathing rates. When he is going to come out of this walk-run gait, he has to give the examiners a minute's warning so that they can catch all his exhaled breath from that last minute for chemical analysis. This alone is quite a comprehensive test of a body under stress.

The test goes on until one of three things happens: (1) the candidate's pulse rate overflows 180 beats per minute; (2) his blood pressure goes past 200; (3) he gives up or collapses. Since most of the men in the competition were in fairly good condition, they seldom terminated because of numbers one or two. It was number three that was likely to give problems.

Before taking the test, I found out that the average length of endurance for our group was about eighteen minutes. The Air Force requirement for a similar test was twelve minutes. Endurance of eighteen through twenty-two minutes was considered a very high score. Twenty-three minutes and above was considered superior. No one in our group had passed the superior mark. I was determined that it would be absolutely necessary for me to gain a superior rating and thus convince the board that I was in as good physical condition as any of the test pilots they were considering. My endurance in sending applications now had to be surpassed on this treadmill.

The end of the story is that I did go for twenty-three minutes and logged a superior rating on this test. It was a tremendous triumph for me. I am sure that if I had been a smoker, I could not have gone that long. This was a test on which I couldn't cheat because they were recording every beat of my heart, my blood pressure, and all the rest. A person might have the physical endurance to just "gut" his way through if he were a smoker, but he certainly couldn't control his heart and the other physical factors being monitored. A number of people collapsed at the end of the test, but I had the satisfaction of walking under my own power down the steps to the table where I was to lie down until my heart came back to normal action.

Besides the physical tests, we each spent three sessions on the padded couch talking to a psychiatrist to evaluate our personality, motivation, and stability. We were told frankly that they were sorting the screwballs from the normals, but they didn't tell us from which group they were choosing the astronauts.

The selection was not concluded with this, however. Through the physical and mental tests the field was narrowed from 3,200 applicants to 63. From here the group had to be cut down to 20 or less. (The final selection was 19.) The technique of the selection board was to look for something that could be used as an excuse to eliminate a candidate. All they had to do was find one fault to throw someone out and thus reduce their number of applicants closer to the 20 for final selection. With this in mind, knowing that if I made one single false move my chances would be zonked, I went before the board for my personal interview.

The board was very pleasant. There was no hostility, just a probing at me for weak spots for more than two hours. All the information regarding my life lay before the board members. There had been a thorough FBI check of each candidate. My FBI reports and letters were all there, until I felt as though I were laying myself out in bits of paragraphs, reports, and references. One of the examiners was checking my very extensive FBI report and perhaps hoping for a weak spot with which to eliminate me.

"I notice, Dr. Lind," he said, "you are very active in the Mormon Church. If you are selected as an astronaut, would you feel that this activity would have to continue?"

There it was. Open? Deceiving? Perhaps lethal? I thought I knew the answer he was looking for. I felt sure that he expected me to say that the only thing that would matter would be the space program, and everything else would be secondary. I wanted to be selected as an astronaut probably more than anything in my life. I felt like a Christian going to face the lions with the choice to either renounce his beliefs and go free or die in the arena. Of course, there was no question in my mind of renouncing my activity in the Church, even for acceptance as an astronaut. True, getting accepted was a pretty big thing in my life, but the Church *was* my life, and I would certainly not compromise it in this vivisection.

My answer: "Yes. I feel that I would certainly have to continue my activity in the Mormon Church, and I don't feel it would in any way conflict with the space program. It has never conflicted in my other professional and military endeavors. I would think anyone with a deep religious background would be a credit to the space program." In giving my answer, I felt sure I had cancelled my chance to become an astronaut.

As it happened, I later became well acquainted with Mike Collins, the fellow who asked me that question, and he is an outstanding individual and a good friend. I think now that my answer was the one he wanted all the time—that I would not forgo my religious beliefs.

Perhaps it is needless to mention this, but let me do so anyway: I was accepted as an astronaut in the NASA program in April 1966.

Chapter 7

Are There "Bounds Set to the Heavens"?

When I was quite young, I dreamed of a life of adventure. I read about Marco Polo going to Cathay, and Columbus discovering America. I thought the big square-rigged sailing ships like the ones that carried such explorers as Magellan and Captain Cook looked wonderful and exciting. But those days were long past. I was disappointed; I felt I had been born in the wrong generation. As far as I could tell, every place had already been discovered and explored, so my generation was doomed to be pretty dull. I had missed the last great age of adventure by two hundred years.

I have since changed my mind. I can't think of a more exciting time to be alive than right now, unless it is the next generation. In the last few years we have been able to go beyond our earth in our exploration—to look at our solar system in a way that it has never been seen before. Surely this is as marvelous and challenging as any exploration of the past. I'm as excited about being involved in exploring our corner of the solar system as I think Magellan and Captain Cook must have been about exploring their corner of the earth.

This is an exciting age in which to be born. Obviously, the space program is one of the things that thrills me about this age. But the fact that the gospel is here upon the earth in this generation is also a very marvelous thing in my eyes. The gospel in its fulness has been available to mortals for a very small fraction of the history of the world. I am very grateful the Lord sent me down during this small fraction of time. I think our particular portion of history is especially interesting and challenging.

The young people of today have grown up with the space program. We have been doing space exploration for some twenty years. My children look at me almost with embarrassment when I tell them I can remember a time when there wasn't a single satellite orbiting the earth. They have that "Oh, father, how old-fashioned" look in their eyes. I had this same look in my eyes when my dad told me he could remember a time before there were any automobiles. Just think what leaps in transportation we have made since my father was a boy! At that time the chief mode of transportation was still horse and buggy—the same as it had been for thousands of years. In the late 1800s, Jules Verne wrote a book entitled *Around the World in Eighty Days.* It seemed farfetched to think you could travel that fast. Yet today you can fly around the world in an airplane in about eighty hours, not days, and a spacecraft can orbit the earth in 91.3 minutes.

I was so thrilled when I was selected to be an astronaut—to be able to help explore space—that it surprised me to find that not everyone felt that way. I received letters from several people saying they were proud of what I had accomplished, but did I feel it was what the Lord wanted? One said that space exploration was much like the Tower of Babel, going where the Lord didn't want his children to go. He said the Lord made this earth for us and did not want us to be concerned with his other creations.

I had, of course, settled this question in my own mind prior to applying for the program, or I would not have pursued this goal. I had prayed and received my

NASA

Don L. Lind, Astronaut

answer, but so that I would have the Church's viewpoint as to this question, I approached President Hugh B. Brown of the First Presidency and asked, "Is there anything in Mormon doctrine, theology, or practice that suggests it is inappropriate for me to try to get to the moon? I want to do what the Lord wants me to do." This was soon after my selection and before we had attained that achievement. The answer he gave me was just what anyone acquainted with the Church would expect him to say. The Father has put us on the earth to gain knowledge, and if getting to the moon and exploring this part of our solar system is an appropriate way to gain knowledge, the Lord would not only want us to learn about this, but would also help us to do it. President Brown said there was nothing wrong with trying to go to the moon. The Church has always taken an enlightened approach toward science and religion.

In section 121 of the Doctrine and Covenants, the Lord tells Joseph Smith (and us) that we are very blessed to live in these latter days and explains why: "God shall give unto you knowledge by his Holy Spirit, yea, by the unspeakable gift of the Holy Ghost, that has not been revealed since the world was until now."

We are living in a day and age when great knowledge is coming forth that has never been here upon the earth before. And people in earlier days longed to have the knowledge that we now have. The Lord continues: "Our forefathers have awaited with anxious expectation to be revealed in the last times, which their minds were pointed to by the angels, as held in reserve for the fulness of their glory; a time to come in the which nothing shall be withheld."

Through modern revelation we will know "whether there be one God or many gods, they shall be manifest." But it is not only religious knowledge that will come forth (although everything unto the Lord is spiritual). He tells us: "If there be bounds set to the heavens or to the seas, or the dry land, or to the sun, moon, or stars— all the times of their revolutions, all the appointed days, months, and years, and all the days of their days, months, and years, and all their glories, laws, and set times, shall be revealed in the days of the dispensation of the fulness of times." (D&C 121:26-31.)

This sounds to me like space research. I believe the Lord is telling us he wants us to learn the laws by which the sun, moon, and stars are governed. He will allow us to find this out now.

Verse 30 speaks of learning whether there are "bounds set to the heavens." When the Lord promises to reveal this, I just get excited thinking about it. That is tremendously exciting because one of the hottest issues in science right now is whether the universe is open or closed. I have an experiment in orbit now that could possibly have a bearing on this question. To be involved in this area of investigation that is inherently part of the gospel as well as part of science is very compelling.

The theory of an expanding universe argues that the universe began with a "Big Bang" explosion. This picture of the universe is based on only two types of measurements. The oldest is the observation that the spectral lines in the light from distant galaxies are shifted in wavelength. Since the shift is toward the red end of the spectrum, we call it a red shift. The explanation proposed by most scientists, although not all of them, is that this is a Doppler effect, which means that the galaxies are moving away from us and are stretching out the wavelengths of light they emit. If all the galaxies are moving away from us, the assumption is that they started from an initial explosion, called the Big Bang.

The second measurement involves the detection of microwaves coming from all parts of the sky. These microwaves have the spectrum that would be emitted from an extremely cold body at the temperature of three degrees above absolute zero Kelvin. They are, therefore, called the three-degree microwave background radiation. The generally accepted explanation is that they came from the Big Bang. The microwaves are supposed to be the original fiery glow that has cooled due to the expansion of the universe until the wavelength is shifted all the way from visual light into microwaves.

My experiment is called the Interstellar Gas Experiment. The purpose of this experiment is to collect interstellar gas particles that move into the inner part of the solar system from farther out. There is evidence that an interstellar wind streams through the galaxy, similar to the solar wind but coming from other stars instead of from our sun. My experiment may become involved in the discussion of the Big Bang theory because if it is successful, we will have the first sample of matter from outside the solar system that we can analyze by running through a mass spectrometer. We will be able to measure the various isotopes of interstellar gas.

My experiment was launched on a satellite that we call LDEF (Long-Duration Exposure Facility), which went into space from the Shuttle in April 1984. It was to be in space for at least a year, then retrieved and brought back to earth for analysis of the data obtained.

Since the Big Bang theory predicts the ratios of the isotopes of the very light atoms, the third line of evidence to investigate this theory has been to measure these isotopic ratios throughout the universe. Up to now, all the samples we have been able to measure directly have come from the solar system—the earth, the moon, the solar wind, and meteorites. Scientists have tried to measure these isotopes from distant parts of the universe by analyzing the light they emit. However, this is very difficult, and the corrections that need to be made are significant. We are trying to obtain the first distant sample that can be measured directly. Our measurements may agree with the Big Bang predictions, but they may also disagree significantly. That is part of the excitement of science. You don't know what your measurements will prove until after you have finished them. I am anxious to know whether our data will suggest our universe began with a Big Bang or "if there be bounds set to the heavens."

My experiment has been designed to capture some particles from the interstellar medium and bring them back to study. If I read President Brigham Young correctly, this is the "stuff" that worlds are made of. He said that someday we "will be ordained to organize matter. How much matter do you suppose there is between here and some of the fixed stars which we can see? Enough to form many, very many millions of such earths as this, yet it is now so diffused, clear and pure that we look through it. . . . Yet the matter is there. . . . Can you form any idea of the minuteness of matter?" (*Journal of Discourses* 15:137.)

It is thrilling to be delving for answers and insights that have been hidden but that the Lord is now permitting to be found. The Lord has always told us that he organized the earth out of existing materials, not created it out of nothing. The Prophet Joseph Smith tells us, "The word create comes from the word *barau* which does not mean to create out of nothing; it means to organize; the same as a man would organize materials and build a ship." (*Teachings of the Prophet Joseph Smith*, p. 350.) We have been told that the Lord did it and why he did it (as a testing place for his children), but not how he did it. Now he may be letting the scientists glimpse a little bit of the how.

Since we are really children of our Heavenly Father, and it is natural for a child to grow to be like his parents, eons from now we too could be "creators." Learning about space matter may be an important thing to know. It is a humbling thought that I am being allowed to play a part, even if only very small. How blessed I feel to be alive today!

The Father tell us in the Pearl of Great Price, "Worlds without number have I created. . . . The heavens, they are many, and they cannot be numbered unto men; but they are numbered unto me, for they are mine. And as one earth shall pass away, and the heavens thereof even so shall another come, and there is no end to my works." (Moses 1:33, 37-38.)

We have observed stars that exploded eons ago as supernovas. These explosions occurred so far away that the light from those ancient explosions is just now reaching our earth. We have detected the expanding shell of debris from even older supernovas. It seems reasonable to me that the Lord uses (or, shall we say, recycles) this matter flying through space from other worlds that "pass away" to organize new worlds. The thought of intercepting, collecting, holding in my hand, and then analyzing some of these particles is not only a scientific adventure, but a humbling inquiry into how the Lord created the heavens.

Chapter 8

Educating a "Man for All Seasons"

Once I overheard one of my children complaining about school. I said to him, "You need to learn to enjoy school because your education never stops. I'm still going to classes to learn things." This startled him, but it's true. When I earned my Ph.D., I thought maybe I was "educated," but I learned that it was only the beginning. What they teach us in the astronaut program alone is enough to make a "Renaissance man" or a "man for all seasons." Besides having to learn the workings of each spacecraft in which we will be traveling, both inside and out (every nut and bolt, as well as computer behavior), we also learn astronomy and celestial navigation. When we were training to go to the moon (and I would have gone if the flights had progressed as was first intended— because of budget cuts, the final three planned flights were cut), we were given the equivalent of a master's degree in geology, with special emphasis on things we might find on the moon.

Those who were candidates for moon flights were taught to fly helicopters because the craft's hovering ability is similar to that of the Lunar Landing Module. The helicopter training was an interesting change from the other flying I do. Usually I am dashing to a planning meeting for NASA or to a youth conference for the Church in a jet going about 600 miles per hour (1,200

Astronauts in desert survival training, wearing burnooses and flowing robes fashioned from parachutes

mph at short bursts if I am in a hurry and throw it in "after burner," but I can't go very long in "after burner" because it gobbles up fuel too fast). In a helicopter, we view the world in a whole different way. We can go slow and even hover over a spot for a time.

We had paramedic training and also went to three different survival schools. The water survival training was designed to teach us how to handle whatever might happen if the spacecraft were to land in the water and we had to evacuate in emergency conditions. In addition, we went to the Navy frogman underwater training school, where we learned scuba techniques so that we could perform underwater simulations of weightlessness. This was fun. The training was in the beautiful waters of the Florida Keys. Every time we dived, the instructor called it "going down with the hungries." Through this training we each became a certified scuba instructor.

There was also desert survival, which took place in

the desert of eastern Oregon. I hadn't realized there was even a desert there or that it could get so hot. During the daytime the sand temperature reached 157 degrees F. This wasn't so fun! We spent all our time just trying to survive. Survival training is essential, since on a space flight, if the spacecraft comes into the atmosphere at even a fraction of a degree off nominal, the landing spot can be thrown off by several hundred miles. If it landed in the Sahara, we would have to try to get by until we were rescued.

Our training was always in groups of three, as it would be if we were part of an Apollo crew. We were given the same equipment we would have if our Apollo crew landed (or crashed) somewhere unexpected. For instance, we had some big parachutes like the ones that Apollo floated down on. In the desert we each cut our parachute up and made an Arabian burnoose for the head and fashioned our own flowing robe. We also made a tent for shade. We learned that the temperature might be 157 degrees F. on the sand surface, but if we were to dig down and cover ourselves with sand, it would be cooler. We created a solar device to distill water.

Jungle Survival School was much more interesting. We traveled to the rain forest of Panama for this phase. The first day was spent in classroom training at the United States Air Force Survival School there. One of the instructors stood out from all the others because of his abilities and personable attitude. His name was Sergeant Duane Hoem. You can imagine how delighted but not surprised I was to find he was also a Mormon. (Scouting and missions seem to develop self-reliant leaders.)

In the display area next to the classroom where we had our jungle survival training were a number of things we might find in the jungle. There were examples of vegetation that was edible, and there were stuffed animals like those we might possibly encounter. Near the

Group of astronauts look over exhibits of jungle artifacts and specimens while training at the Panama Jungle Survival School. Arrow points to Don Lind

ceiling were several large tree branches draped with two huge stuffed boa constrictors. As Charlie Duke, one of the astronauts, and I stood talking during one of the breaks between classes, I was startled to look up and see the "stuffed" boa just over Charlie's head stick out its tongue. The boas turned out to be *live* snakes, but the instructors had very carefully not mentioned that detail to us. The next morning when we got to class the snakes weren't on their tree branches. We had to wrestle them out from behind the radiator where they had gone for warmth! The instructors took them off to the officers' quarters mess, and later that afternoon we had the snakes for lunch. They really didn't taste bad if we could forget what we were actually eating.

In one of the lectures, the instructor said the concern about snakes in the jungle was highly overrated. There wasn't a chance in ten thousand that we would see a snake in the wild at all, because they were so few and far between. Within an hour after he said this, one of the instructors came in very excitedly and reported that a coral

snake had been found at the edge of the grass that surrounded the school building. It was the largest coral
snake any of the instructors had ever seen. We all went
out to see the deadly coral snake, and I mentally said to
myself, "Well, that's my one chance in ten thousand. I
won't see any more snakes."

However, on the third day out in the jungle, as we
were moving down the trail on our way out, we had a
fright. The trail was steep and slick from the rain, making it very difficult to maneuver around and maintain
our footing. Another group of astronauts had gone
down this same trail about ten minutes earlier. We were
moving along the edge of a moderate-sized stream. I was
the second person in line, behind Fred Haise. Suddenly,
and without a word, Fred leaped out into the stream and
began to point frantically at the ground near my feet. As
soon as I looked where he was pointing, I joined him in
the stream, but unlike Fred, I made a lot of noise. I
shouted to the others to watch out for the snake on the
trail. It was a seven-foot fer-de-lance, a large and extremely venomous viper that we had been told was the
most dangerous snake in the Panamanian jungle. Its
venom can quickly paralyze a man.

The third person in line was Ralph Morris, a photographer from *Life* magazine who usually went with us on
our expeditions. He was absolutely terrified. He joined
me in the water and yelled, "Let's get out of here before
someone gets killed!" One of our Panamanian guides
and a flight surgeon from NASA Flight Medicine managed to pin the snake's head down with a forked stick
and to put the snake into a burlap sack. Then we started
to argue. Since the snake was a pit viper, it could strike
only at things it could see; and since it was dark in the
sack, it wouldn't strike at anything. The guide said it
was perfectly safe to carry the bag. However, I didn't
want to be the one to carry it, just in case I got a snake
that hadn't heard the rules.

Bruce McCandless, one of the astronauts, carried the snake out of the jungle and took it to Panama City. There he put it in a wire cage and brought it back to the United States. At the airport, the U.S. Customs officer told Bruce he couldn't bring the snake in. But Bruce had looked up the regulations beforehand, and he quoted to the man the paragraph that said pit vipers could be brought into the States. The Customs officer checked and found that such was the case—if the snake didn't have some kind of infection in its ears. He asked, "How do I know it's clean?" Bruce handed the man the cage and said, "Here—check him." The Customs agent backed away, exclaiming, "No, no! He looks clean to me!" So the snake was allowed into the country. The fer-de-lance was given to the Houston Zoo Viperarium.

When I came to Texas, I thought I had seen the absolute maximum rate water can come from the sky, but in the rain forest I found that a Texas gully washer was just a gentle spring shower. We had been dropped by helicopter into the rain forest south of Lake Gatun, the water source for the Panama Canal Locks, and were setting up camp. We had been advised to set up at least eighteen feet higher than the very small stream along which we were camping. The first day the rain wasn't too bad, but the next afternoon we had a real storm. The rain came down so hard I could hardly believe it. We even discussed whether we might be inhaling a dangerous amount of water that was condensing in our lungs. We had built a pretty sturdy palm shelter so we weren't directly in the rain. Yet the air was saturated with water particles.

As a Boy Scout I had learned to trench around a tent, and I had done a pretty commendable job (by Boy Scout standards) around our shelter. But the water was pouring down the hill at such a rate that it was a solid three inches or more deep. My little twelve-inch trench hardly even fazed or deflected it. Water in the bottom of

NASA

Don Lind, left, and other astronauts eat exotic foods during jungle survival training

our shelter was three or four inches deep and gushing through. The three of us sat together on top of the table we had made (weren't we glad we had made it sturdy!). Within only ten or fifteen minutes the formerly small streambed had risen by about fifteen feet and was forty feet wide. We had spent all morning chopping down two trees, which were eighteen inches in diameter and about seventy feet high. The storm literally washed them away. They floated down the stream a short distance and became wedged sideways. For just a brief minute the water rose another four or five feet from the blockage, and then the trees shattered in two and were washed downstream. When we went down the stream the next day, we couldn't see even a trace of the trees anywhere.

Our Panamanian guides were experts at using the machete. We could say, "Build a bridge," and in twenty minutes they would have a bridge built. I saw one of

Group of astronauts and other NASA pilot trainees prepare to jump off floating platform during survival training

them take the bark off a tree just as fast as he could swing the machete, and every chop was literally in the previous chop, and a little lower. We couldn't take a ruler and make a straighter, narrower line than he made as he peeled that bark off the tree and rolled it out to make a mat.

The machetes that the astronauts used in the jungle were terrible, however. Rather than buying them for about five dollars in Panama City, which would have been the easiest thing to do, NASA designed its own special machetes. They were made to some very unrealistic specifications, one of which was that they had to be able to soak for twenty-four hours in salt water without rusting, which meant that they had to be made of stainless steel, which meant that we couldn't sharpen them. The designer had also come up with the idea that if the knife had sawteeth on one side, it could also be used as a saw. But instead of making U-shaped teeth, he used V-shaped teeth, which meant that at the bottom of each V was a stress point.

One morning we broke three machetes trying to cut down the big trees. I was swinging one of them as vigorously as I could, trying with my dull knife to compete with a Panamanian wielding a sharp one. Jack Swigert, who had been working with me, sat down to rest against another tree fifteen or twenty feet away. Suddenly I realized that there was no more machete—nothing left in my hand but the handle. I looked over at Jack, who had turned white as a sheet and was staring up at my machete blade stuck in the tree about a foot above his head! We were the first group to use this type of machete, and you can imagine how we reported on its effectiveness. The astronauts are often used as guinea pigs to try out new things. We hoped this particular situation would never happen again.

We received medical training when we were preparing for Skylab. For the Skylab missions, the crews would be in orbit for as much as a month or two at a time, so there was the possibility that someone might get appendicitis or have an impacted wisdom tooth, or something of that nature. The question of whether to abort a multi-hundred-million-dollar mission because of some health problem could not even have the *chance* to arise. Medical problems we could solve on orbit were discussed with us, just in case such problems arose in flight. Actually, we couldn't do anything like an appendectomy in orbit (though we learned how to do it on the ground) because in weightlessness it would be extremely complicated to keep body fluids in the abdominal cavity; they would want to float away. But we learned how to care for a considerable number of minor medical emergencies.

At Shepherd Air Force Base we started going through medical training similar to that which might be given to a paramedic who was going to some remote place, such as up on the Dew Line, someone who could be snowed in for nine months and who might have to do an operation on the wardroom table. We had some special medical textbooks that were more simplified by far than those that most medical schools would have used. In other words, we could take a symptom and look up in a sort of "cookbook" all the various tests that should be run and the procedures that might be used. In space we would never, of course, have done anything without first consulting with doctors on the ground, but we couldn't ship up a doctor to do the job. If blood samples had to be drawn, we were the ones who had to be able to do it. We learned to do throat cultures and read analyses of them, and how to sew up our fellowmen, practicing a lot on sponge rubber until our technique was pretty good. Then we went to the Texas Medical Center and worked with five specialists who gave us more detailed assignments, such as checking peoples' ears and eyes, taking blood pressure, and giving shots.

As a sort of final exam, we went to two sessions in the emergency rooms at Ben Taub Hospital, the charity emergency hospital in Houston. We worked on the Saturday night midnight to 8:00 A.M. shift. We saw quite a few fight victims and were given plenty of chances to sew people up. One woman whom I assisted had a badly lacerated arm. I asked her how she had done it, and she replied it had been a fall. I asked sympathetically, "When did this happen?" She answered, "Right after he hit me." (In addition to some medical training, I was exposed to a different side of life than I had seen before.)

The most interesting case I saw involved a young man from the psychiatric ward who, in a fit of despondency, had broken a light bulb and tried to slash his throat. We had to do a full operating-room procedure. He had made absolute mincemeat of everything between his chin and his Adam's apple. Under the very careful supervision of the surgeon on the case, I sewed all the muscles of his throat back together so that he would have all the proper facial expressions. Then we started sewing tissue back together. The surgeon started at the left ear and I started at the right, fastening tissue together and moving toward each other until we met in the middle. I was going to count all the stitches we put in, but after several hundred I stopped counting. We spent several hours before we were done and could bandage the patient up.

A few weeks later I went back to Ben Taub Hospital for another shift. I wanted to see how the young man was doing, so I asked to go to the psychiatric ward to visit him. He looked quite good—I was proud of my handiwork. As we turned to leave, another patient who was suffering from delirium tremens rushed up the hall and flung himself at me, yelling, "Doctor! Doctor! Help me!" I looked around, wondering where the doctor was. It took only a minute to realize that to him, anyone wearing a white suit was a doctor.

I'm afraid I felt a long way from being a medical doctor, but I had done a surprising number of things I never thought I could do. My wife says she is glad to have me in her "year's supply" of first aid and other emergency supplies, that I come in handy. I've even done some dentistry. At Wilford Hall Hospital at Lacklin Air Force Base in San Antonio, we were taught to pull teeth. One retired general came back three times so he could say he had had an astronaut pull his teeth. The people we worked on had to sign a statement that said essentially, "I know this man is an incompetent, but I still want him to pull my teeth. And I won't sue anybody, no matter what happens." The first tooth I had to pull really turned out to be oral surgery. I gave the patient a mandible block shot and then proceeded to pull a wisdom tooth, which was somewhat impacted. After I got it out, I had to suture the jaw, which was swimming in blood. It turned out fine.

As you can see, astronauts learn to do many things that the average physicist rarely gets to do. But they are skills that could be lifesaving if needed in orbit.

Chapter 9

Geology Training for the Moon

One of the things that is professionally satisfying about the space program is the technical and scientific training we are given to go along with our various assignments. Back in the Apollo program, those of us who were candidates to go to the moon received a very sophisticated course in geology, giving us the background to interpret and observe accurately geological structures that we might see on the moon. It was not a particularly balanced course in geology, because we did not do any oil exploration or other experiments that concern geologists here on earth. It was really astrogeology.

We were not sure what we would find on the moon. The crews who would go there were to bring back sample rocks and many pictures, but they could not bring much of the moon back for scientists on earth to study. Thus, the astronauts needed to be trained well enough that they could recognize the different kinds of geologic structures they might see. They would also need to be able to tell which of the rocks might be best to bring back as lunar samples. Our next-door neighbor, James Irwin, who went to the moon on Apollo 15, found and brought back an orangish-colored specimen that the scientists dubbed the "Genesis Rock"; they believe it was probably one of the oldest found.

To prepare us for lunar flight, we were given fabu-

*Astronaut Don Lind
studies geology map
during geological field
trip*

lous training in geology. If there was an example here
on earth of something we might find on the moon, we
studied it. We had classroom study with the finest
teachers and then took field trips to the best available examples of what we were studying. We visited volcanoes
in Hawaii and Iceland, observed a rhyolitic ash flow in
the Valley of 10,000 Smokes on the Katmai Peninsula in
Alaska, studied stratification in the Grand Canyon, and
climbed in a huge meteor crater in Arizona.

We started with two general field trips to examine
stratigraphy, faulting, and folding, which we did not expect to see on the moon but which were very good background for the kinds of things we would see. We went
to the Marathon basin in West Texas to look at some of
the structures there. Then we went to the Grand Canyon
of the Colorado, which is one of the best examples of
stratigraphy in the world. We went to the South Rim and
spent one entire day hiking down through the canyon,
studying it layer by layer all the way down. Our instructor first gave us an orientation lecture to introduce
the subject. Then he gave us a more detailed lecture on

each structure as we came to it, such as the Coconino sandstone, the Great Red Wall, and the Toroweap. Two astronauts and a geologist would go as teams of three through each particular structure and take samples; then we would pull off to the side of the trail for a detailed analysis of what we had observed. By this means we worked our way to the floor of the Grand Canyon, having had graduate-level lectures right there on the trail. After staying overnight at the Phantom Ranch, we went back up to the rim the next day by mule train.

We were all in fairly good condition, but we always had a few camp followers, photographers, and reporters who went along. I remember one photographer said to me, "My editor doesn't believe I do things like this. He called me up and gave me this assignment, but he didn't tell me what to expect or what I'd need. And here I am in a business suit and definitely not hiking shoes." He had so much trouble that we ended up carrying his camera pack and other gear for him. I stayed with him behind the others just to make sure he made it to the Phantom Ranch. It is a much harder hike than many people who start expect it to be. One man we met on the trail was so exhausted that he offered a thousand dollars to anyone who would get him out of the canyon alive.

One of the things we expected to see on the moon was basaltic lava flows, so we went to the Pacific Northwest to study the great Columbia lava flows. We went through lava tubes, which are formed when a large pool of molten lava is slowly moving. The moving current keeps fluidity while the rest solidifies, forming a tube of molten lava that flows out under a solid lake of lava. As the last lava flows out, it leaves a big hollow tunnel. Sometimes the tunnels are miles long.

We also expected to see the equivalent of shield volcanoes on the moon. The best example of this on earth is on the big island of Hawaii. There we studied Kilauiki, the vent in the volcano Kilauea that is most active. I remember reading a story about President David O. McKay's visit to Kilauea volcano in 1921 when he was on a worldwide tour of missions. He reported that he and his companions were chilled on their backs by the cold wind, but the heat almost blistered their faces as they watched the molten lava in the fiery pit below them. One of the elders discovered a volcanic balcony about four feet down inside the crater from which they could watch the display without being chilled or roasted, so President McKay and three elders climbed down into this to watch the volcanic display. Suddenly President McKay said, "Brethren, I feel impressed that we should get out of here." Just as they reached the rim, the whole balcony crumbled and fell with a roar into the molten lava far below. I thought of this as I watched the steam venting from this same place. Even when a volcano is not erupting, it is impressive and can be dangerous.

Another thing we expected to see on the moon is a maar, an explosive kind of volcano. The best example of that in the Americas is in the Pinacate volcanic area in Sonora, Mexico. We had all kinds of problems getting into there with our equipment, and the Mexican officials gave us a hassle. But the biggest problem was cholla cactus. I am convinced that cholla cactus will jump about a foot to get you if you turn your back on it. Some fairly spectacular minor surgery had to be performed on some of the astronauts who backed into cactus. One spine became embedded in the corner of my thumbnail, and I had to pull it on through the edge of my finger rather than back it out because of the barbs.

In Iceland we studied fissure volcanoes. We discovered that the Lord has not finished creating the earth yet. In Iceland it is still being formed. The island of Surtsey was formed in 1963 when a new volcano erupted in the ocean off the coast of Iceland. Our trip out to see this was fascinating. In only a couple of years it had changed from red hot lava to an island with plants grow-

NASA

Don Lind studies crystals in basaltic rocks during field trip to Mexico

ing on it. Iceland is made up of volcanoes, with about thirty considered active. The national geologist, Sigudur Thorarinsson, was recruited to lead our expedition into the interior of Iceland.

NASA has a rule that no more than a certain number of astronauts may fly on any one airplane, so that a crash would not wipe out the entire astronaut corps, so we flew into Iceland in two groups. I was on the group that arrived a day early. Our hosts had arranged for us to go sailplaning. It was fun but a bit embarrassing to me, because when you fly a jet you hardly ever use the rudder, but in a glider it is used almost all the time. The man I was flying with was always chipping away at me to use more rudder. When I climbed out of my sailplane, the man who landed right after me was astronaut Joe Engle. I said, "How did you do, Joe?" He answered, "Well, not too good. The guy was all over me about not using enough rudder." I thought that if one of the best test pilots in the United States (he tested the X-15) had the same problem I did, then maybe I shouldn't feel too bad.

When the rest of the astronauts arrived, we went out in the field to study volcanoes. One of our modes of transportation was a bus that was specially designed to go through streams and over lava fields. We had to cross a number of very wide but shallow rivers. The driver was an expert on the interior of the country. There usually were no roads, and the terrain changed often as rivers rose and fell and dirt was washed away from a formerly solid spot, leaving a big hole the bus could sink into. The driver would get out of the bus frequently and poke down in the water with a big metal pole—plumbing to see how deep it was.

We stopped at a place called Landmannalaugar, a meadow at the foot of a big escarpment formed by an advancing lava flow. Immediately adjacent was Vatnajökull, a glacier that covers a large section of Iceland. Melting glacial water ran down through the meadow, forming a very cold stream. Running into this same riverbed was steaming water that had percolated down through the volcanic escarpment. Thus, there was water just above freezing at the bottom of the stream and a layer of hot water on the top. We were told that the technique was to dive in and thrash wildly to mix the two streams of water. My initial dive was absolutely spectacular, because for the first half-second I was boiling and then I was freezing. This sort of entertainment that went along with our geology study was always an important part of the education. In college they call this extracurricular activity, but we liked it, whatever it was called.

On the moon we expected to see a *nuee ardente*, a particular kind of rhyolitic ash flow. One of the best examples of this is in the Valley of 10,000 Smokes on the Katmai Peninsula of Alaska, the stubby end of the Aleu-

Astronauts and instructors surround Icelandic Prime Minister Bjarni
Benediktsson (left center foreground, in gray sports coat) during geology
training in Iceland. Arrow points to Don Lind

tian Islands. This was an extremely interesting trip.
Robert Smith from the University of Arizona, the world's
expert in egnimbrites, the rock that this kind of ash
forms, came to Alaska and taught the class. It seemed almost incredible to sit around in a fishing camp and have
high-level college classes. During the day we were taken
out by helicopter to the volcanoes and lava fields. Then
we'd return to the lodge and sit around the table for a
very sophisticated graduate-level course in geology.

The people who ran the fishing camp baked huge
trays of brownies and cakes for us, and as we sat listening to the lectures, we munched constantly on goodies.
The average weight gain on that one-week trip was over
seven pounds. We came back like fat little boa constrictors that had just swallowed the yearly pig.

I had an interesting experience going into Alaska.
Some of our friends were managing the lodge at Glacier
Bay National Monument in the Alaskan panhandle,
northwest of Juneau, so I took some leave and went a
few days early to visit them. Juneau sits essentially in a

very narrow box canyon. The FAA approach plate into Juneau is the only one I have ever seen that says you have to establish visual contact with the ground ten or twenty miles south of the airport and then fly in with visual conditions, because a plane cannot turn around in the canyon. You have to land on the runway, taxi to the far end, turn around on the ground, and take off in the opposite direction. There is no such thing as a missed approach to this airport.

At Juneau, I learned that I was to fly on to Glacier Bay in a pontoon plane. The entire cabin area where I had expected to sit was filled with boxes of groceries, and I was instructed to climb over these and get into the co-pilot's seat. The pilot said over the radio, "Okay, Hank, I'm on my way," started the engine, and off we went. Now I didn't have a radio so I couldn't hear the response, but it was obvious to me that the pilot had not received an instrument clearance and had not gone through the procedures that I was acquainted with. He flew over close to one side of the canyon, banked the plane up, turned as tightly as he could, and headed for the back of the box canyon. The cloud layer was low enough that I wasn't sure he could get over the end of the canyon without going into the clouds, and he obviously did not have an instrument clearance. But it turned out that there was a clearance of a few hundred feet between the clouds and the ground at the head of the canyon.

The plane popped out over the edge and over the tundra, where there was a little more clearance. Then the pilot pulled out an aviation chart; he was obviously flying radio ranges. Now, radio ranges had not been used in the United States for a number of years, but here he was, trying to tune his little "coffee grinder" radio receiver to pick up the radio range. He would hold the headset close to his ear and try to tune it, then beat on the radio a couple of times and try to tune it again. Finally he threw the headset down on the floor. To me, every lake below us looked like every other lake, and I thought we must be hopelessly lost, but he knew exactly where he was going and flew us straight to Glacier Bay. After a delightful visit with our friends, I went back to Juneau the same way I had come.

In Juneau I reported in at the airport for my flight to Anchorage. According to my ticket, I was to leave at 1:30 P.M. on Pacific Northern Airways. But when I checked in, the agent took my baggage and told me the flight would leave at 6:10. I asked, "What do you mean, 6:10? I have a confirmed reservation on the 1:30 flight!" He replied, "Well, I'm sorry, but that flight does not exist. It won't exist until the runway is finished at Ketchikan."

My problem was clear-cut. If I didn't leave until 6:10 P.M., I would not arrive in Anchorage in time to make my connection to King Salmon at Katmai and then on to the Valley of 10,000 Smokes. I would miss a whole day of geology training if I was delayed. I even went to the Air National Guard to see if they could or would fly me out, but they were unable to.

Then I learned that a Cordova Airways flight was scheduled to leave fifteen minutes before the Pacific Northern Airways flight. Here I learned a lesson, too late, never to do something out of spite. Because I was upset, I insisted on having my ticket and luggage transferred to Cordova. I was still seething when I climbed on the plane. Soon I found I was in a situation I'd rather not have been in. The plane was an old DC-3, and there were six other passengers, all swathed in fur parkas and mukluks. They were all going to a place called Yakutat, a very small village at the beginning of the Alaskan panhandle. I was the only one going on to Anchorage. As we neared Yakutat, the pilot announced that it was fogged in; he would fly in a holding pattern for one hour, and then if the fog did not lift, he would have to go on to Anchorage. So we started flying around and around, waiting for the fog to disperse or the hour to end.

When we first got on board the aircraft, the steward-
ess passed out plastic glasses to everyone and proceeded
to fill them with champagne. When I declined her champagne, she slithered into the seat beside me and wanted
to know, with a pout, why I wouldn't take any. I still declined, so pretty soon she went away to refill the other
cups. Soon they got to be a very merry bunch, the stew-
ardess included. My seat was near the galley, and every
time she went back there, I could see her drink right
out of the champagne bottle. When one was empty, she
would get another one. When she went up into the cockpit, which she did frequently, she still had that bottle in
her hand.

All the passengers except me were now roaring
drunk and singing wildly. I soon became convinced that
the pilot, too, was drunk, because when we went into
the holding pattern over Yakutat, he was doing strange
things with the plane I did not understand. I realized
that in all probability, I was the only sober person on the
aircraft! I was very seriously thinking of trying to force
my way into the cockpit and taking over the controls,
but I decided against that. I knew how to fly a high-
performance jet plane, but I had never flown a DC-3. I
knew that if I even dinged a wing tip, I would be put in
Leavenworth prison for air piracy, so I decided that was
not a reasonable option. What I did was to go around the
plane, gather up every pillow that was not in use, and
pile them around me, building an absolute barricade in
front of me. I tightened my seat belt, said a few prayers,
and reviewed all the crash techniques I had ever heard
of, all to the merriment of my drunken fellow passengers. Amazingly, the pilot brought the plane in with
hardly a bounce. I got up out of my seat, trembling, and
walked off that plane resolving I would never again do
anything out of spite.

When I finally got to the fishing camp near the Valley
of 10,000 Smokes, I had missed the first day of geology,

so Dr. Smith took me up on Mount Katmai and gave me
a private, personal class. One of the interesting things
we saw was very lightweight pumice rocks that were actually lower in density than water, floating on top of the
water in the lake.

At the camp I had an experience that humbled me. I
was sharing a cabin with Astronaut Jack Lousma, and I
asked if he would mind leaving the light on a few minutes so I could read. He agreed because he also wanted
to read. I was in the top bunk reading an Alfred Hitch-
cock mystery, and when I got tired, I leaned over the
edge of the bunk to see if he was ready to turn off the
light. That was when I discovered that Jack was reading
the Bible. It humbled me to see him setting a better example for me than I had been setting for him, though I
always do say my prayers, no matter where I am or
whom I am with.

We were sure we would find an impact crater on the
moon, and the best preserved example of this kind of
crater on earth is the Barrington Crater in Winslow,
Arizona. The geologist who had done by far the most
extensive geological survey of that crater was Gene
Shoemaker, who was head of the Astro-Geology Section
of the U.S. Geological Survey. Once again we were
given on-the-spot training by the expert, standing on the
rim of the meteor crater and then climbing down inside.
This was particularly interesting because it was something we would surely find on the moon. The lack of atmosphere on the moon allows meteors to strike the
lunar surface without being burned up, so the moon is
pockmarked with the resulting craters. Most meteors
that come near the earth are burned up by heat caused
by the friction of the atmosphere, and as a result, not
many actually hit the earth.

There is a theory that when a large meteor hits the
moon, it causes a splash of moon rocks into space. Some
of these go flying out so fast and far that they are caught

in the gravitational pull of the earth, hitting it in a strewn pattern, similar to the way a handful of pebbles would fall if you threw them together. This is one of the theories of the origin of tektites. Most tektites look much like flat glass beads. Their chemical makeup is not from the earth. The dictionary defines a tektite as "a glassy body of probably meteoric origin and of rounded but indefinite shape and unknown origin." They appear to have been heated to a high degree twice—once when the meteor hit the moon and again when the friction of earth atmosphere heated them as they came in and were strewn over areas of the earth. This is the theory that Dr. John O'Keefe of the Goddard Space Flight Center advocates. Soon after I was selected as an astronaut, I was at a party with Dr. O'Keefe. He took my hand and placed one of his precious tektites in it with the admonition, "Take this with you to the moon. Carry it in one hand and keep picking up rocks until you find one that matches it, and don't come back until you find one!" I wish I could have done that. But my trip to the moon wasn't to be, so the tektite still sits in my drawer, and the knowledge of astrogeology is tucked away in my mind. Who knows, someday I may use it yet.

Chapter 10

Safety—and
Heart-Stopping Moments

When I joined the astronauts and became part of the space program, one thing I found very comforting was that NASA took almost extreme concern for the safety of the crew. This covered all phases of the mission, both ground and flight operations. With several million pounds of propellant in the booster rockets, even ground operations could be hazardous. The first time I saw the preparations that had been made for even the remote possibility of an explosion on the pad, I could hardly believe I was really part of this "Buck Rogers" world.

If there were indications of an imminent problem after the crew had boarded the spacecraft atop the Saturn V rocket, the whole launch complex would go into an emergency procedure. While the crew scrambled to unbuckle themselves from the seats and open the command module hatch, the swing arm with the "white room" (the dust-free entrance room where you board the spacecraft) would be moved back by remote control to surround the command module hatch. If there was a fire in the area, the crew could quickly activate a sprinkler system that would envelop the white room, the swing arm, and the upper level of the gantry in a water curtain. By the time they reached the top of the elevator, it would be in position with the door open. As soon as they touched the button for any floor, the elevator would descend at high speed to the second level within the mobile launcher, where they would be behind five inches of steel armor plate.

Once the elevator snapped open, directly ahead of the crew was a tube three feet in diameter into which they could dive. Actually, the tube was a seven-story-high slippery slide. You came out of the bottom of this tube going thirty-five miles an hour into what we called the "rubber room," so-called because all the surfaces were covered with three and a half inches of sponge rubber. During the critical last phase of the Saturn V launch countdown, as many as fourteen people might be on the gantry, including the crew. The rubber padding at the end of the slide was placed there so fourteen astronauts and technicians wouldn't be injured as they came tumbling out of the escape tube.

Immediately opposite the slide was a round steel door that looked like the classic bank vault. This was the entrance to a large steel sphere suspended on railroad springs. Since it was located two stories underground, it could withstand the explosion of all the propellants of the rockets and spacecraft on the surface above. The possibility of an explosion was remote, but if it did occur, it would be gigantic. The crew and technicians might have to spend as much as twenty-four hours in the sphere before they could be rescued, so food, oxygen, and padded couches were provided. The couches had seat belts so they could strap themselves in, since the earth would shake from such a powerful explosion.

Another safety factor that they had for both the Mercury and Apollo astronauts was the launch escape tower. (The Gemini rocket fuel was not as explosive, so they didn't use an escape tower for this program.) The tower was a long, very powerful rocket that sat on top of the command module as the command module perched atop the booster rocket while on the launch pad. If there was danger of an explosion in the rocket below the com-

mand module or if, on launching, the spacecraft veered
off course, then the launch safety officer at mission control would have to destroy it before it could hit Miami or
some other place. If either of these things happened, it
would be important to get the astronauts away before
the rocket blew up.

All that the commander in the capsule had to do
was to rotate the hand control that usually went up and
down. The rocket on top of the command module would
then fire and pull the module free from the rest of the
booster and carry it on a high arching curve to a position
one mile above and one mile to the side of the explod-
ing rocket. There the crew would deploy the parachutes
used for recovery and float down, splashing down in the
ocean, where they could be rescued by boat.

Today, the escape mechanism used for the Shuttle
while it sits on the launch pad is a half-mile-long guy
wire with small pulley cars attached. If there is a crisis,
the crew members get out of the Shuttle quickly, jump
on the small cars, hit a release for the cars, and go flying
down the guy wire. By the end they are traveling at
about sixty miles an hour. The cars are stopped by a big
net. The astronauts then jump out of the cars, run over a
small hill, and get into a cement and steel bunker located
there.

People sit up nights trying to think of every problem
that could go wrong and figuring out how to handle
each one. But even with all the preparations and planning, we have still had our share of heart-stopping moments.

Someone wrote a hymn for the astronauts. The first
part goes:

> O God, Creator, in whose hands
>   the rolling planets lie,
> Give skill to those who now command
>   the ships that brave the sky.
> Safely pilot all who seek to find
>   their haven through the sky.

It has always been my prayer that the Lord would watch over us. We have known there were dangers in space exploration, but we have felt, and still feel, that the risks should be taken to do what needs to be done. When Ed White, the first man to walk in space, was once asked what was worth risking his life for, he said, "My country." He was unashamedly patriotic. I feel this way too, and I liked him for it.

The first U.S. orbital mission took place in February 1962. As John Glenn was orbiting the earth, the controllers on the ground had indications that the heat shield of *Friendship 7*, John's space capsule, might be coming loose. Without a heat shield, not only will the spacecraft burn up from the friction of the atmosphere, but astronauts will too. They recommended that John leave the retropack on throughout the entire reentry, hoping it would help hold the heat shield until air pressure could keep it in place if there was a problem. The retropack wrapped around the edges of the heat shield and held the retrorockets, and once the rockets were fired, the retropack was supposed to be jettisoned. Now the controllers were telling him not to jettison it. He was at a very critical point in the mission. He had to concentrate on firing the retrorockets to slow him down and take him out of orbit, but he also had this new worry that he might not have the protection of a heat shield.

As John fired the retrorockets and then entered the atmosphere, the friction and ionization built up so there could be no more radio communication with the ground. The sky, formerly black, began to glow with flaming orange. That was the heat shield starting to burn up from the tremendous friction from the speed of reentry. It had been designed to burn off layer by layer, vaporize, and dissipate the heat into the atmosphere. But all John could see through the windows now were flames—he was inside a fireball! He knew that some of this would happen, but he hadn't expected to see huge burning chunks flying past his windows. The capsule started

buffeting, and John thought the heat shield was breaking up, crumbling, and flying away in flaming chunks.
He expected any second to be feeling the heat himself
and that would be the end. It takes real courage to be the
first man to face an unknown danger.

As it turned out, John Glenn landed in safety. The
heat shield, except for what had been intentionally ab-
lated away, was intact. The chunks of flaming debris had
apparently been the retropack burning up and breaking
away. The telemetry to the ground had given wrong indications about the heat shield's being loose. The heat
shield had done just what it was intended to do—keep
the heat on the outside. On the outside the shock wave
reached 5,400 degrees F., while only a few feet away,
where the astronaut sat, it was only about 75 degrees F.

John commented after his reentry, "There are going
to be sacrifices made in the program. We have been
lucky so far." Gus Grissom said, "If we die, we want
people to accept it. We are in a risky business, and we
hope that if anything happens to us it will not delay
the program. The conquest of space is worth the risk."
(James C. Hefley, *Lift-off*, Grand Rapids, Mich.: Zondervan, p. 76.)

On that fateful Friday in January 1967, no one sus-
pected trouble when Gus Grissom, Ed White, and Roger
Chaffee stepped into their Apollo capsule for a routine
simulation. All went fine for about four hours. Then at
6:31 P.M. a voice suddenly cried from inside the capsule,
"Fire aboard the spacecraft!" Before the three men could
be rescued, they were asphyxiated.

Shock waves from the tragedy jolted the entire space
industry and delayed other Apollo flights until the
spacecraft could be redesigned for the utmost in safety.

After the death of the three astronauts, Major General Edward H. White, Ed White's father, wrote to his
twelve-year-old grandson: "Your father . . . believed that
the exploration of the universe must and will go on, that

it is our destiny as children of God to keep seeking new challenges, asking new questions, finding new answers. He knew that the farther we go, the more mysteries we encounter. But this only proved to him the infinite power and majesty of God." (Hefley, *Lift-off*, p. 77.)

The three astronauts were not in space at the time of the accident. It happened at Cape Canaveral in the Apollo capsule at the top of the rocket as it sat on the launch pad. This was one of the final tests as the launch date approached. The atmosphere they were breathing in the capsule was one hundred percent oxygen at 16.5 pounds pressure. A broken wire caused a spark that ignited the interior of the spacecraft, and pure oxygen at such high pressure caused materials to burn that no one expected would. Even the insulation on the wires burned. The investigation board went over everything with a fine-tooth comb. They found that even if the men had had a little more time, they probably would not have been able to escape because of how the hatch was latched. The hatch opened inward and took ninety seconds to open. As a result of the investigation, it was redesigned to open outward in only three seconds.

We don't use pure oxygen in the space capsule any more, and everything possible has been made fireproof. Millions of dollars were spent to develop a lightweight fireproof fabric for our flight suits. The developers and planners had tried to do things safely, but sometimes they didn't know what the dangers were.

We astronauts and our wives attended each sad funeral, and for months afterwards we lived under a pall of sorrow that some of our group had to pay the ultimate price. We didn't stop, though. We pulled ourselves together and went on. But I remember the feelings I had a few months later when Kathleen and I visited the Cape and stood near the spot where our friends had died. There was a sense of sadness, but also a resolve to go on and not let their lives be lost in vain. We felt a spirit of national pride as we stood there, almost as though we were at a shrine, the way I feel at the Lincoln Memorial in Washington, D.C.

The meticulous search for causes and better ways of doing things after the fire made it much safer for all future crews. Gratitude is not an adequate word for our feelings.

When lightning struck the Apollo 12 as it was being launched from Cape Canaveral, I was the assistant capsule communicator. During a space flight one person communicates with the crew onboard the spacecraft. This person is always an astronaut because we speak the same language. He is called the Capcom (for capsule communicator), and all messages are relayed to the crew through him. Astronauts rotate the shifts as capsule communicator, but during critical mission phases, at least two are on the console together in Mission Control.

At this blast-off I was assistant to Jerry Carr, the prime communicator. At 36½ seconds after lift-off, the spacecraft was struck by lightning. There were no significant indications of any lightning in the clouds, and actually there wasn't any. What happened was that the exhaust plume from the engine, which is a conducting plasma or gas, had simply discharged the cloud to the ground.

At the first lightning discharge, we completely lost telemetry with the crew. Several sensors were damaged, though none were very significant. We were left without communication because the electrical load was automatically dumped onto batteries and all equipment nonessential to sustain life was cut off the line. On the ground we knew something was wrong, but we did not know what.

At 52 seconds the spacecraft was struck by a second bolt of lightning. This strike didn't do much damage except to bite into one of the words in the computer. But this particular word was rather critical, because it was in the program that told the computer how to keep the

NASA

Astronaut Don Lind erects the sunshield on a mockup of a central station, a component of the Apollo Lunar Surface Experiments Package, under simulated lunar gravity conditions

inertia platform from tumbling. Because this platform is the sensing element that enables the computer and the spacecraft to know which way it is going, it is absolutely indispensible for flight. It is mounted on gimbals in such a way that it is possible to hit the endstops on the gimbals and thus tumble the platform. The computer watches to make sure this does not happen. But the computer's interpretation of the change in the word was that the gimbals were in gimbal-lock, whereas actually it tumbled the platform while trying to prevent the platform from doing that very thing. So at this 52-second point, we were without electrical power and without a meaningful computer.

As soon as we found out what was happening, we got telemetry back from the crew. We then had to ascertain whether or not the crew could sustain life for the

next few moments, because if there had been some critical damage like the rupture of the pressure vessel, a different kind of action would have been required. But we
attained a successful orbit, as history shows, and had the
time to carefully evaluate the situation. From there the
mission went on to be a success.

After Apollo 12 we figured that nothing could be
more exciting (or should I say tense). But then came
Apollo 13, when an explosion destroyed one-sixth of the
spacecraft when it was two-thirds of the way to the
moon. Miraculously Mission Control got the men back
safely. I later suggested to Ed Mitchell, our next-door
neighbor, that his Apollo 14 crew should not try to top
13 for excitement. We don't know whether the crew's
hearts could have taken it, but we are very sure the controllers' hearts could not!

My wife and I were in Washington, D.C., to speak at
the festivities during the Cherry Blossom Festival when
the Apollo 13 crisis started. The Church was providing
much of the entertainment during the festival. Since we
had lived just outside Washington, D.C., before joining
the astronaut corps, we had looked forward to going
back. We were at a gathering of friends when the announcement came over the news that Apollo 13 was
having trouble. I glued myself to the radio. The newscaster was saying things like, "It doesn't look too bad,"
but behind his voice I could hear the hook-up between
Mission Control and the space module, and I could tell it
was very much more serious. At that point the commentator didn't know how serious it was, but I knew the
meaning of the terminology they were using. He was
just reporting what he was told.

As soon as our part in the Cherry Blossom Festival
was concluded, we hurried for home in Houston, feeling
a need to gather our children into our arms of safety.
After seven years of waiting, our family of five children
had recently been increased to six by a dear baby girl,

Lisa. We didn't want to be away from any of them. They knew the other astronauts in the program and their children and might be wondering, "Could this happen to my daddy when he goes in space?" We wanted to be there to answer their questions and be closer to the source of answers.

Jim Lovell, Fred Haise, and Jack Swigert, the Apollo 13 crew, were about two-thirds of the way to the moon when they heard a loud bang. Jim said later, "We've had similar sounds in the spacecraft before that meant nothing . . . and then I looked out the window and saw this venting. . . . My concern was increasing all the time. I went from 'I wonder what this is going to do to the landing on the moon' to 'I wonder if we can get back home again.' . . . and when I looked up and saw both oxygen presssures—one actually at zero and the other one going down—it dawned on me that we were in serious trouble." (From NASA, Apollo 13 Mission Report, "A Successful Failure.")

Jim's assessment was accurate and, if anything, optimistic. The bang they had heard was the explosion of liquid oxygen tank number two in the service module. This tank provides the vital oxygen on which fuel cells number one and number two relied to generate the electric power to operate the systems in the command and service modules. The fuel cells were the primary power source for the spacecraft.

NASA has made most things redundant, so if one thing goes wrong there is another thing to do the job, but no one could ever have guessed that there would be a time when one-sixth of a spacecraft would be blown up while in outer space. There was a back-up battery-powered electric supply in the command and service module with a lifetime of about ten hours, but Apollo 13 at the time of the explosion could not get home in less than eighty-seven hours. You can't just turn around and fly home. The craft was more than 200,000 nautical miles out in space with a dead service module, including its main propulsion engine. The initial trajectory of Apollo 13 was what is called a "free return" course. Such a trajectory, if undisturbed, would carry the spacecraft behind the moon, out again, and on a correct course back to earth. On their way from this trajectory they had switched partway out to a hybrid course that would land them on the moon where they had been planning to go; now they would have to switch back to the original course. But each action took precious power, of which there was so little.

While the astronauts aboard the damaged spaceship set about powering up the lunar module that would now be their "home," or lifeboat, Mission Control at the Manned Space Center in Houston started mobilizing help. The manufacturers of the major systems in the lunar and the command and service modules combined were asked to get their top specialists immediately available to provide answers. Many worked around the clock for days. The engineers and their simulators and computers at North American Rockwell were helping, as were the experts at Grumman Aerospace Corporation, makers of the lunar module, and people at TRW Systems, who built the descent propulsion engines. The lunar module was going to be asked to do many things it had not been built to do, with a coast-to-coast network of experts, computers, and simulators hooked together to find out how to get the men home.

The command and service module's ten hours of operating life had to be reserved for the approach to earth's atmosphere. After the lunar module was powered up, the command module was shut down completely. Later all the lunar module's systems except those relating to life support and communications were turned off. By these thrift means, the lunar module's consumables meant for two men for fifty hours (if used on the moon) were stretched to provide life support for three men for eighty-four hours.

NASA

Don Lind practices getting into
and out of lunar module mockup

The ride home was pretty cold. With the command module shut down, there was no internal heat source. The command module was 38 degrees F., and the lunar module was not much warmer. It took the men three breathtaking days to get home, days of innovation and jerry-rigging to make things work. Canisters of lithium hydroxide "washed" the atmosphere in the spacecraft of carbon dioxide produced by the crew's breathing, but the canister system was overloaded because three men were breathing there instead of two, as was intended if the system was used on the moon's surface. Thus, the carbon dioxide in the cabin atmosphere began a potentially dangerous rise. Lovell was able to rig an adapter by hand that would allow him to attach a hose from the lunar module to the additional lithium hydroxide canisters in the command module. This hose went through the docking tunnel and had to be spliced to make it long enough.

Necessity is truly the "mother of invention." It wasn't a comfortable ride, but, as Frank Buck used to say, we were able to "bring 'em back alive." After intensive simulations on the ground, Mission Control radioed up to the crew a phased power-up sequence in which all needed systems were operable for only two and a half hours prior to reentry. The crew had to go into the command module and jettison the lunar module before reentry. Catastrophe had been averted, and in the end the Apollo 13 space capsule was brought into the most accurate landing of any of the previous twenty-two space flights. It splashed down in the Pacific just three and a half miles away from the recovery aircraft carrier, and only one-fourth mile from its target point. The rescue mission had taken 86 hours and 57 minutes from the time of the explosion. The whole world had been united in prayer for the astronauts' safe return. What a joyous shout went up as we watched on television the three orange-striped parachutes blossom within view of the carrier, gently bringing the astronauts to a safe landing in the quietly rolling ocean.

A few friends later asked me, "Now that you know how dangerous space travel is, are you going to quit?" I said, "No, indeed! Now that I know how safe it is, I'm going to continue on!" Can you imagine going out to the parking lot and finding that your car had exploded, destroying one-sixth of it? Would you expect to be able to drive it away? I think not. Yet there are so many safety features built into the system, and so many capable people working for our safe return, that when this happened to a spacecraft almost a quarter of a million miles away, the astronauts could and did bring it home safely.

Chapter 11

"The Eagle Has Landed"

When I finished the fundamental training we go through as astronauts, I was involved in some of the early parts of the Apollo program, which was the program to put American astronauts on the moon. My first assignment was in lunar surface operations. This meant that one other astronaut and I were to supervise the development of equipment and establish the procedures to be used while the crew was on the moon. A package of scientific experiments called ALSEP (Apollo Lunar Surface Experiment Package) was to be deployed by the first astronauts to go there. This was to be left on the lunar surface and would send back data to scientists on earth for a year or more. One of my main assignments was to supervise the development of ALSEP, which required a seemingly endless series of design reviews and planning conference meetings all across the country.

Sometimes I had to get into a pressurized space suit and work through the experiments or procedures to see what could or could not be done in the suit. The pressure suit is very constricting and seems to have a mind of its own. If it isn't made exactly to your measurements, it doesn't want to bend where you do, and sometimes I would come out of it with big welts where it "bit" me.

Nevertheless, the space suit is a remarkable piece of equipment. It is a pressure vessel capable of keeping the astronaut alive out in the very hostile environment of space. For example, on the moon the temperature goes from 212 degrees F. in the daytime to − 270 degrees F. at night. The suit is twenty-two layers thick, one layer of which is a network of tiny tubes through which a coolant flows to help prevent the astronaut from becoming over-heated as he goes about his tasks. Each space suit costs $26,000, but if it saves a life, it's worth every penny.

Sometimes the tests were performed in the Water Immersion Facility, known as the WIF (pronounced wif). I would put on the pressure suit and the assistants would attach lead weights to me so I wouldn't float to the top. Depending on how much weight they put on me, they could simulate either the total weightlessness of outer space or the one-sixth gravitational field of the moon. This procedure is called becoming neutrally buoyant. As I worked around, deploying the experiments, I would almost feel weightless, except for a little viscous pull of the water.

While working in the WIF, an astronaut always has to have several other persons with scuba tanks down there too. If he tears a hole in the pressure suit, water will come in. Because he is weighted down with lead weights, he can't get to the surface and so he could drown. The other people are there to get the weights and helmet off quickly so he can use a scuba mask and tank of oxygen. The WIF tank is eighteen feet deep, and if the astronaut were to come up too fast, he could get the bends and possibly die. A decompression chamber or tank is right beside the WIF. I'm glad I never needed to use it, but it has been used on occasion by others.

The most common way to simulate weightlessness is in the KC-135 (the Zero-G aircraft). This is a big, empty plane with padding all around the walls, floor, and ceil-ing. The pilot is strapped in (fortunately!), but the other people in the plane are not. The pilot flies a parabolic loop maneuver so that the centrifugal force of the parabola balances five-sixths of the gravitational attraction of the earth. This creates the same one-sixth gravitational attraction that he would experience on the moon. A person really does float as he goes over the loop. This lasts for twenty-two seconds. Then for some strange reason (since the plane is now in a nosedive), the pilot insists on pulling up. He will do one parabola after another like a huge roller coaster.

Floating in weightlessness is fun—the 250-pound space suit and backpack don't seem to weigh anything. But as the plane pulls out of the dive and up again, it's something else! A person is pushed down with double the force of gravity, and he feels as if he's being squashed by 500 pounds. After about forty parabolas, his stomach says, "I wasn't meant for this!" and he has to get the helmet off quickly because he's going to throw up.

I practiced performing the procedure of setting up ALSEP in the Zero-G aircraft, but the task had to be chopped up into twenty-two second segments while we were in the one-sixth G mode. We timed to see how long it would take to do each task on the moon, and then we wrote the instructions and timeline for the astronauts who went to the moon to use it.

I remember how I felt the first time I saw the Apollo Saturn V that would take man to the moon—the first time men would leave earth's orbit and visit another sphere. I had gone with some other astronauts to Cape Canaveral to look over this vehicle that had been designed to lift some of us into outer space, and I had read the specifications rather carefully. I knew the height of the entire structure (364 feet); I knew the thrust of the engines (7.5 million pounds in the in the first stage). I knew that it was assembled in the world's largest building (one huge room, 525 feet high—so high that clouds have been known to form from condensing humidity and it has even rained inside this building); and I could

quote you the statistics on the size of the gigantic cater-
pillar Crawler Transporter that had to carry it out to the
launch pad on the beach. Each tread shoe of the Crawler
weighs a ton; there are fifty-seven treads or shoes on
each track; and there are eight tracks per vehicle. The
Crawler stands five stories high. (This is the same vehicle that carries the Shuttle to the launch pad today.)
I understood—quite well, I thought—the magnitude of
this project.

At the Cape, the rocket out on the pad looked kind
of unimpressive because there was nothing nearby with
which to compare it. As we drove out toward it, it got
bigger and bigger; but even when we got to it, we didn't
appreciate the size. It was like trying to view the Empire
State Building from the sidewalk just below. We rode
in the elevator inside the umbilical tower to the crew-
loading platform (you get there by pushing the "43rd
floor" button).

When I stepped out on the platform from which the
astronauts board the space capsule and looked down on
that huge vehicle and then around the area, I felt absolutely overwhelmed! For the first time I really caught the
magnitude of this spaceship and what we were doing.
The thought came to me that the first stage of the rocket
held 4.5 *million* pounds of propellant—and at lift-off this
would burn in two minutes and thirty-one seconds at a
rate of fifteen tons per second! If you look at your car's
carburetor, you know that the fuel line is smaller in cir-
cumference than your little finger. In the Saturn V there
were *ten* propellant lines in the first stage, each the size
of a bushel basket. You can imagine how impressed I
felt. But the most impressive thing was the fact that they
were planning to put me on top sometime and push the
button!

I think I probably knew more about what Neil
Armstrong and Buzz Aldrin were to do on the lunar sur-

face than they did, because I had spent about two and a half years developing all those procedures and working out the tests on the hardware they were to use. They had not been able to spend much time on lunar procedures; most of their time and training concerned how to get there and back in safety.

I was in the NASA control room during the first moon landing in order to talk Neil and Buzz through the deployment of the lunar experiments if they should have any problem. They knew how to do it if all went right, but they had not learned how to handle any malfunctions of the equipment. All went well with this part of the mission, and I had an opportunity to see firsthand what I think of as one of the great days in all history: the day that headlines in papers all over the world read "MAN ON THE MOON!"

If you were watching the landing on TV in July 1969, I don't know how much of the excitement you sensed when we landed Apollo 11. In the control room where I was, the tension was electric. As the lunar module finally touched down, the capsule communicator announced, "The Eagle has landed!" Astronaut Charlie Duke was the man in the control room on the ground who communicated with the astronauts on the moon. He told them, "Congratulations! We've got a bunch of blue people down here." They didn't understand what he meant, but it was almost literally true, because everyone had been holding his breath from the tension of the last couple of minutes, fearful of what might happen.

When the astronauts started their descent, we didn't know what kinds of problems they were going to encounter. One scientist had seriously proposed that the surface of the moon was covered with a mile-deep layer of dust and that the spacecraft would settle right out of sight. We sincerely hoped this wouldn't happen. We were quite sure it wouldn't, because the unmanned Sur-

Don Lind deploys an umbrella-like experimental folding antenna, designed to relay lunar surface data and communications back to earth

veyor spacecraft we had sent up had not disappeared. But we didn't know if they would encounter enough dust to stir up such a cloud that they couldn't see to land.

When we fly our NASA jets, we are required to be able to visually see the last 200 feet ceiling to ground and last quarter mile horizontally before we can land here on the earth. We simply cannot land a plane, even at an airport with all the electronic facilities that can be built and a crash crew standing by in case anything goes wrong, if we cannot see the last 200 feet vertically and the last quarter mile horizontally. But we had nobody to prepare the place for us on the moon. The Marines and Seabees had not volunteered to go up ahead of the astronauts to lay down matting so they could land on a nice, prepared runway. The astronauts were going to have to land on unprepared terrain.

For the landing site, we had picked the flattest spot on the front side of the moon. The landing ellipse, or area where the computer was going to put them down, was 5.7 miles long and about two-thirds that wide. About 98 percent of that area was quite acceptable for landing; however, there were also several thousand small craters within that landing ellipse.

We didn't know if Neil's vision would be obscured so that he couldn't see to land, and there was no crash crew and no electronic landing system. So we didn't know what was going to happen when that spacecraft came in to land on its four spindly little legs with what looked like snow saucers as feet. If you land with one saucer on a rock you sort of roll over, and that is considered very bad form in our office. You see, it makes the lift-off very difficult, pushing the moon ahead of you.

We had built the lunar module somewhat like a helicopter in the sense that we could come in and hover and look around for a landing spot if the computer had not done very well picking the spot for us. It is one of the perversities of orbital mechanics that if we are going to land on the front side of the moon, we have to fire the engine on the back side of the moon; therefore, the engine must be fired by the computer. We do not find out until about three minutes before touchdown where the computer has sent us. If it has sent us into an unacceptable spot, then we could bring the lunar module in to hover while we looked around for a few thousand feet in every direction for a better spot to land. The problem with this is that it uses a lot of fuel.

The spacecraft was built rather frugally as far as weight goes. We didn't want to lift more weight than we had to. We were not able to send much extra fuel for that kind of a maneuver because it would take one thousand pounds of fuel to get just one pound to the moon. Thus, we were able to send only enough extra fuel for 60 seconds. This means that we were going to fly from here clear to the moon, 239,000 miles away, with only 60 seconds of extra fuel! Imagine driving clear across the

United States with only enough extra gas in the gas tank for one minute more of driving—providing you don't dig away from a single stop sign on your way from here to there. That is the kind of fuel situation faced by the astronauts going to the moon, but there was nothing else we could do.

Another thing that gave us pause was that the lunar module was built to operate in the gravitational field of the moon—but it had never been tested. This may seem like a considerable oversight, but the problem was that we could not simulate the gravitational field of the moon for something as big as the lunar module trainer. With smaller things we could simulate potential situations in the Zero-G aircraft or the Water Immersion Facility, but there was simply no way to test the lunar module in the environment in which it would have to operate. What we had to do was test it in the environment of the earth and then hope that none of the engineers had slipped a decimal place in making their conversions. But we would never really know until we got there.

In a way, this was similar to my first experience flying jet planes in the Navy. If something goes wrong with a jet, the easiest way to get to the ground is to eject and simply come down with a parachute, which is the standard procedure. But because I did not want to eject the very first time under an emergency situation, I asked the Navy for permission to do some practice parachute jumping. This was to help prepare me so that if a problem arose, I would have a little experience in the parachute part of the ejection. But my superiors rejected my request. They had spent $260,000 to teach me to fly, they said, and didn't want me laid up in a cast for six months if I made an unsuccessful jump. According to them, there was no such thing as a practice parachute jump. Every single one is for real. There is no way to jump out of an airplane and have it just for practice; it has to work the very first time, and each time thereafter.

In the same sense, the lunar module had to work the very first time without ever having been fully tested. So as you can imagine, many things combined together to make that day when the astronauts on Apollo 11 were setting down on the moon's surface a very exciting one.

As luck would have it, when the spacecraft came around from the back side of the moon on the orbit that would land it, the computer had it headed straight for a big boulder field. The astronauts knew they couldn't land there; and with only 60 seconds to hover, find a better place, and then land, they were in a difficult situation.

I flew jet aircraft carrier landings in the Navy for four years, and I can guarantee that if I were within 60 seconds of fuel-out and didn't have my wheels firmly on the carrier deck, I would be well into cardiac arrest. With 60 seconds—one minute—left of fuel, the astronauts in the spacecraft were 420 feet in the air, flying about 50 miles an hour and trying to overfly this boulder field. We on the ground didn't know why they hadn't landed (they weren't very talkative). Buzz Aldrin was the only one saying anything, and he was just calling out the altitude velocities from the radar altimeter. At 30 seconds they were still 220 feet in the air, trying to slow down so that they wouldn't skid into a landing.

When the spacecraft finally touched down on the moon, according to our calculations there were only 13 seconds of fuel remaining. Now it turned out that when the fuel stopped sloshing around in the tank and we could read the gauges more accurately, there were really 42 seconds of fuel left, so it wasn't a big deal after all. No wonder those of us in the control room at NASA were all blue in the face from holding our breath. The viewing room right behind and overlooking the control room was also filled with tense people. The only ones who

were not frozen with fear were five visiting con-
gressmen; they didn't know what was going wrong and
didn't dare ask.

Some people have speculated that Neil Armstrong
was selected to be the first man to walk on the moon because he was a civilian, but I don't think that is why he
was chosen. The way crews in the space program are
selected is a mystery even to the crews themselves, but it
is my personal opinion that the main reason Neil was
chosen was because he had had four major accidents in
his flying career, including two that involved NASA and
the space program. Now that really may not sound like a
very good recommendation, but it was how he handled
himself during these crises that counted. He proved that
when he was seconds away from almost certain death he
still was clear-thinking "Mr. Cool." He could operate
with amazing accuracy and calmness under the most
trying conditions. NASA management knew that if anyone could go to the moon and get out of trouble through
intuitive reactions and cool thinking, it was Neil
Armstrong. This trust paid off, because when he came in
during those last few seconds before touchdown, he did
very well under the most trying conditions.

As Neil and Buzz began their assigned tasks on the
lunar surface, I found it difficult to believe that what I
watched on the television monitor was really happening
239,000 miles away. It felt to me as though they were
going through yet another training session on the earth.

It should have been easier for me to accept the reality
of what we were watching than it was for most people.
Hadn't I, for over two years, represented the astronauts
in the development of the equipment and the procedures that were being used on the lunar surface? I had
tested the equipment, rehearsed the deployment
schemes, and tried out the timelines. I knew what Neil
and Buzz were to do just as well as they did. Yet it was

still difficult to fully believe that what the United States had been working toward for almost a decade had finally been accomplished. Men were working on the moon! I remember how I felt that night as I stood outside my home with my family, looking up at the moon and realizing some of our friends were up there. I think we all felt goosebumps.

This was a tremendous achievement. It was also an impressive example of how a nation, when it has a specific, clearly defined goal and the will to unite and work toward that goal, can accomplish almost anything.

I was a child during World War II. Now, war is terrible, but it sometimes does accomplish one good thing: It mobilizes a nation to work together for a common goal, that of liberty and safety of home and family. The biggest strides forward in technology often take place at such times. People are willing to sacrifice comfort and ease for the good of all. There was one Christmas when none of us got toys; we got savings bonds instead. All metals and rubber were going into defense projects, so many household items, cars, and toys were not being built. We felt that we were all in this together, and we were glad to work for the cause.

I believe that the space program, particularly the Apollo moon project, sparked the common interest of the nation and gave us a cause. It mobilized the forces of technology more than ever before. The list of inventions and techniques developed for use in the space program that are now commonly used in our daily lives is impressive. Just a few of these are weather and communication satellites that keep us informed of world conditions; hospital equipment that uses remote sensors, developed for astronauts in space, to monitor the vital signs of patients; the whole microcomputer industry; and natural resources monitored from space. For instance, blight in a cornfield can be detected earlier from an infrared photo than it can be by a county agent standing in the field looking with his natural eye at the corn leaves themselves.

The fact that we were in a space race with the Russians gave us added incentive, an almost wartime impetus, to be the ones to get to the moon first. We took pride in what we were doing, and we worked together to make it happen. This seems to me to be a much more civilized way to unify a nation and make great technical advances than to kill people, as happens in war.

Reaching the moon had been an extremely difficult technological challenge, and there were setbacks and frustrating delays, such as the tragic fire in which Gus Grissom, Ed White, and Roger Chaffee were killed while training for the first Apollo flight. That delayed the Apollo schedule by about a year. There were some naysayers at that time, critics who claimed that the spacecraft had little chance of working properly and that the risks were entirely too great. There were literally millions of problems to be solved. And yet, despite all this, as I stood at the capsule communicator's console in the control room, Neil and Buzz were actually walking on the moon, collecting geological samples, and setting up scientific equipment. The president of the United States had set a goal, and tens of thousands of Americans had helped accomplish it. The magnitude of our working together unitedly gave me as much pride as the deed itself.

I am sure that this principle applies also to our personal lives. If we choose our goals and work toward them earnestly, we can accomplish unbelievable things. But without specific goals, we can spend much energy spinning our wheels and getting nowhere. We might have our own "fire" of adversity along the way, but if we don't give up, we will achieve the end we are seeking.

There are several necessary steps in applying this principle. Let me describe how I have seen the process operate in my life, drawing on my goal to become an astronaut.

The first step in goal-setting is to choose an attainable objective. The goal can be difficult (we develop much more if it is), but it must be realistic. For example, the chances of my becoming an astronaut were really very small. However, I did have experience in flying jets from a Navy carrier, and I had completed a good education program in science. At least I had a chance. If I had set a goal of becoming a Metropolitan Opera star, there is just no possibility that I would have ever attained that, as I am sure my friends who have heard me sing can testify.

Another step is to start early. This is particularly important for achieving such goals as a college education, or a mission, or a temple marriage. We need to set these goals while there is time to complete all the preliminary preparations. When NASA called for applications for scientist-astronauts, it would have been far too late for me to have started on my Ph.D. classes or on my flight training.

The next step, and perhaps the hardest, is to make sure that we do everything we can to reach our goal. We will need the blessing of the Lord and perhaps the help of others, but without our own efforts, we have no chance. In my case I knew I had to pass a difficult, competitive physical examination, so I started running two miles each evening for conditioning, as well as going through a daily calisthenics program. Fortunately, I had lived the Word of Wisdom all my life, so that gave me an edge over those who smoke and drink. Also, I needed more jet-flying experience; through the Naval Reserve, I was able to increase my flight time to well above the minimum level.

I knew that certain areas of scientific background were particularly desirable. One of these was geology, a subject I had not studied, so I took an evening class in

geology and included this as part of my other college rec-
ords. There is one delightful thing about such preparations: Even if we do not quite attain our goal, we are
much better off for having tried.

The final step is persistence. After some of the
Apollo delays and setbacks, critics of the program
wanted us to quit because they said it was too hard and
required too much of our national effort. I recall that
when I was learning to play the piano and when I was
learning German and calculus, it was easy to get discouraged. Progress seemed so slow, and I was not sure I was
getting anywhere. It took three and one-half years of
persistent applying to NASA before I was accepted for
the astronaut program. I was told no officially, formally,
and finally more than a dozen times. I suppose I am just
stubborn, but each time there was another chance, I
would try again. In the meantime, of course, I kept up
the physical fitness program, the flying, and the studying.

Finally all the effort paid off: I received a call inviting
me to join the space program as an astronaut. The goal
had been achieved!

When Neil Armstrong reported that "the Eagle has
landed," the United States had shown the world that the
sky is not the limit. Likewise, if we individually choose
wise goals and put our very best efforts into achieving
them, we can accomplish things that right now may
seem impossible.

Chapter 12

Making Decisions under Pressure

As I participated on the sidelines during the first har-
rowing landing on the moon, the thought came to me
that in a very real way Neil Armstrong was all alone.
There were thousands in the communication net, probably the biggest assemblage of talent available in the
communication links that we had ever had working together in the world, yet there was only one man in the
whole system who had his hands on the controls. He
would either do well or he would crash, depending on
his own ability. What he had learned and trained himself
to do was going to count right now. He did very well,
but in doing it, he probably felt terribly alone. It was just
him or no one. Many times during our lives we each find
ourself in situations that can be compared to this, where
we feel terribly alone.

As I have gone around the Church speaking at youth
conferences, young people tell me that they often feel
this way. They are faced with important decisions, but
they feel frighteningly alone in making their choices.

Now in another way, Neil would be the very first one
to admit—and indeed, he would insist—that he was
simply the apex of a tremendous team. A lot of people
were behind him who could help, who had helped, and
who would help if required, plus a great many people
were wishing him well. For example, Buzz Aldrin was

standing eighteen inches to Neil's right, breathing a bit
erratically and sincerely hoping Neil would succeed in
landing the spacecraft safely. In addition, a lot of people
back on the ground were pulling for him. Some were
even in a position to help.

In the last 60 seconds before touchdown, the computer sent twelve messages to the crew. Now when you
talk to computers, you usually type things on a keyboard, but this particular keyboard writes out numbers
on a green display panel. Twelve times in that last 60
seconds it wrote out the number 1202, which one would
normally look up in a book of messages to find out what
it was saying. But in the training he had gone through,
Neil had memorized what 1202 meant years before, because of the significance of the message. What 1202
means, in essence, is: "The computer has failed. You are
on your own. Good luck."

What happened is that we had built a radar altimeter
so incredibly accurate that every time we flew over a
rock that was more than one meter in height, it would
change the altitude, call up the computer, and tell it,
"Hey, you have a new altitude." If the computer got
more than 1/1000th of one second behind in its calculations, the 1202 light went on. With the altitude in error
by only a few meters because of the size of rocks they
were flying over, the correction would be changed im-
perceptibly, so it was totally safe to ignore that particular problem. Neil had even been told ahead of time that
if any caution warning lights came on during power descent, he was to simply ignore them. If anything of real
importance came up, ground control would call him and
let him know.

On the ground was a man whose job was to ascertain
when the 1202 lights could be ignored. If they could be
ignored, he would say nothing, but if anything was
wrong, he would speak up. Neil had to decide whether

*A popular youth speaker,
Don Lind talks to a group of
Scouts*

this man was really telling him that everything was all
right, or the man was confused and didn't know what to
say, or perhaps he had gone out for a cup of something.
The people who were giving him advice were giving the
advice by simply being silent in this particular moment.

Sometimes we each find ourselves in situations
where in one sense we are desperately and tragically
alone, and in another sense we have a lot of people sup-
porting us who can and will help us if we want to listen.
These kinds of situations are what I call "the Neil
Armstrong situation"—when we are faced with decisions, challenges, or temptations where what we do is as
critical for a period of our life as what Neil did was critical
for that particular flight.

Most of us reach a stage in life where we have to
make really pivotal decisions that will affect all eternity.
The most important decision we will ever be asked to

make is the one we made in the council in heaven before the world was. Had we not voted properly at that time, we would not be here upon the earth now.

I believe that the second most important decision we make in all eternity is whom we will marry. Based on that decision, all sorts of other things follow, such as the genetics of our children, where we will live, and our whole lifestyle during mortality. In fact, if I interpret the scriptures correctly, our very salvation is influenced by our marriage choice, because we enter the celestial kingdom only two by two, as into Noah's ark. If we marry a millstone, we can't drag her or him in. Thus, we need to make that decision very carefully and prayerfully.

Another important decision that most youths have to make, one that is not quite as important as whom they marry but nevertheless is an important decision, is what they are going to do professionally. But suppose a person has a job that he really doesn't do very well and it doesn't give much satisfaction. He doesn't get much out of it, and he drags around just enduring it. He can't complain to the boss, so he goes home and nags his wife, which is the wrong thing to do if he wants his marriage to last forever. Life can turn out to be unpleasant if we get into the wrong job, so this is a very important decision.

Throughout life we make choices and decisions almost on a daily basis that determine our status with the Lord. In the late teens and early twenties we probably face more of these challenges than at any other time in our lives. For example, when I was in my early twenties, I faced military service. I went off to Navy boot camp, which is kind of a dismal prospect. Finally I got my first weekend pass. I was going to get out of that unpleasant place, at least for a few hours. Suppose some new buddy that I had just met said, "Come on. I know a *great* place!" Now, "great" places near Navy boot camps are usually *not* where our mothers want us to go. We have to make the choice: do we go off with these newfound friends and get into who knows what kind of trouble, or do we spend the weekend alone in the barracks? Our decision can have a profound effect on our lives.

Another example: Say we go off to college. We would really like to get into a sorority or fraternity, and we are invited to a rush party. It is important that we make a good impression, or we won't be asked to join. Before we realize what has happened, someone thrusts a cocktail glass at us. Now we have to decide what to do with that first cocktail. Do we pour it into a potted palm? (It might make the palm even more potted.) Do we drink it? Or do we hand it back and try to say something gracious as we decline it? If this is the first drink we have been offered, and it comes when we are under the stress of wanting to feel accepted, we are going to face a decision—and we may feel as desperately alone as Neil Armstrong felt.

When I was growing up in Salt Lake City, there was an area behind the state capitol building that was known as "passion flats." (Now I'm not confessing I know about it personally, just from hearsay.) If you're a girl, imagine the following situation: You've finally gotten a date with a great-looking guy you've been eyeing for a long time. Suddenly you find he is pulling into "passion flats." You can imagine that in the next few minutes you are going to face some challenges and choices that could significantly affect your life, even your hereafter—and you are going to feel all alone in making your decisions. It is going to be hard to remember that you have a mother, a Laurel leader, a bishop, and a seminary teacher who are all rooting for you to make the right choices.

These are the kinds of things I'm referring to when we are getting into the "Neil Armstrong situation," a dichotomy in which in some ways we are all alone and at the same time we have a big team behind us to help. I would like to suggest three things that we should do as we face such decisions, challenges, and temptations.

1. We need to decide whom we are going to listen to. Lots of people are willing to give advice, and we can't possibly follow all of it. So one of our important decisions is whom we are going to listen to, because some of the advice will be contradictory. Some of the worst advice we will ever get is from friends. Think about that. How much advice do we take from our enemies? None. We don't listen to it. So the only advice we do get is from our friends. Some of that may be excellent, but some of it is bad advice, and we have to sort it out. There may be those who would like to recommend to us the use of alcohol, tobacco, or drugs, or who might make suggestions that will place us in compromising situations. But even if they are friends, they may not necessarily have our best interests at heart. We have to decide whom we will listen to. The person who offers us the first sugar cube with LSD on it (and the first cube is always free, of course) may not be the best person to advise us about the dangers of drugs.

When I was in graduate school, to help make ends meet, I took a job flying with the Naval Reserve, flying out of Alameda, California. Occasionally we were asked to furnish services for exercises with the North American Air Defense Command. We would fly off in our A-4Ds to some place like Tonopah, Nevada, then turn around and try to make a simulated bombing run on San Francisco before the defense command could get F-106s from a nearby Air Force base up for a simulated rocket run on us. Our job was to see if we could penetrate the air defenses. We pulled all the dirty tricks we could think of, and we did everything we could do to foul up their system.

One time when we were heading for San Francisco and knew that things were under way, we switched our radios over to what we knew would be the operating frequency of the F-106s. For a few minutes we heard nothing; that was while the Air Force pilots were running out to their planes, getting them checked out, and taking off. Soon an eager young voice came over on the radio channel and said, "Torchy, Torchy! This is Lover Boy Two. Airborne, standing by." At that time Torchy was the code name for the radar site on the north side of Mount Tamalpais. Lover Boy Two was the code name for the first F-106 that was airborne, and he wanted instructions. Since you cannot transmit UHF (ultrahigh frequencies) through Mount Tamalpais or any other solid object, for that matter, and he was taking off on the opposite side of the mountain, nobody was able to talk to him until he got to about 5,000 feet. But we didn't want that eager young pilot to become despondent with no one answering him, so we came up on the air and told him, "Lover Boy Two, this is Torchy. Angels, Three zero zero"—which means climb to 30,000 feet headed straight west. In just a few more minutes a third voice came on the frequency and cried out, "Lover Boy Two! Lover Boy Two! This is Torchy! Reverse course! Reverse course!"

Well, that pilot wasn't going to be fooled by any old Naval Reservist (or so he thought). He was going to stick with that nice friendly voice that had been talking to him from the ground up. So he ignored the second voice and pressed on, headed straight west. Keeping in communication with the pilot, we ran several simulated rocket attacks on some Naval Reservists out over the Pacific, but he never did see them, because they (we) were really 500 miles the other direction, between Tonopah and San Francisco.

After a while the pilot reported, "I'm bingo," meaning "I have just enough fuel to make it back to the base." We switched him over to the real recovery frequency and he was directed back to land. Then we landed at Alameda and filled out reports, adding, "Ha, ha! Look how we fooled you!" The point was that "Lover Boy Two" was getting all the advice he could ask for, from a voice that sounded friendly. The problem was, the advice didn't come from somebody who had his best interests at heart. So we all have to decide whom we are going to listen to in life, because sometimes bad advice will come from friends or someone who sounds like a friend, and we need to recognize this.

2. We should never be intellectually embarrassed about putting our faith in principles. Sometimes young people think that the principles are unsophisticated or that they are old-fashioned, and they may feel a little embarrassed about hanging on to the things that their parents, priesthood or Young Women adviser, or seminary teacher talk about. An experience from my professional background illustrates why I think it is good and intellectually acceptable to have faith in and hang onto principles.

During World War II the scientific community was involved in what was called the Manhattan Project, which was the first development of atomic energy. I later got my Ph.D. in high-energy nuclear physics, but I was still a boy when the Manhattan Project was going on. One of the problems the scientists faced at that time was a nuclear process called beta decay. This is when a radioactive nucleus blows itself up, for reasons known only to the nucleus, and spits out a bunch of fragments of that nucleus. One of the fragments is a high-speed electron called a beta particle. Under the rules of nuclear physics, these particles have to be spinning, but there was not as much spin after the disintegration as there had been before. Essentially, the particles had lost a half unit of angular momentum, or spin. Until the scientists knew why this was happening, they didn't know how to control it.

Enrico Fermi, one of the great nuclear physicists, suggested that the scientists had simply not detected one of the particles that came out of that little explosion. If they found the missing particle, he said, they might also find the missing half unit of spin. Dr. Fermi at this time was a naturalized U.S. citizen, but emotionally he was still an Italian, so he gave the supposed particle an Italian name: neutrino, which means little neutral one. The properties of the neutrino are as follows: It has no mass. It doesn't weigh anything. It has no electrical charge. It has no magnetic moment. Its cross-section, or ability to bump into things, is so close to zero that to stop a neutrino by putting mass in front of it to make it bump into atoms would take several light years. Thus, a neutrino can whistle clear through the entire earth with almost no chance of bumping into anything on the way through.

The scientists said to Fermi, "Oh, we understand. It's sort of nothing spinning"—implying that if he wanted to take two weeks' vacation, he would probably feel much better afterwards and would forget the neutrino. But Dr. Fermi persisted. He said, in essence, "I believe in the principles called the conservation of energy and the conservation of angular momentum. Every experiment ever conducted on this subject by man suggests that those two principles are true. And if those principles are correct, the neutrino must exist, no matter how stupid it sounds. Let's start looking for it." Well, the scientist not only found the neutrino, but it now comes in several "flavors," a total of six different kinds. Now everyone says, "Oh, we always knew they existed," but they really didn't always know they existed. They were discovered only because Dr. Enrico Fermi believed so strongly in the two principles involved that he was willing to postulate the absolutely preposterous particle called the neutrino—and he was even willing to take a considerable amount of ridicule over it.

The mental processes Dr. Fermi went through aren't really different from the process a young woman might go through if she is at a sorority rush party and says to herself, "Let's see, this morning when I was thinking clearly, I decided I would observe the Word of Wisdom at all times. Alcohol isn't good for me. Maybe I should just hang onto that principle. I won't tell these sorority girls about the Word of Wisdom right now, because they would just laugh, but I'm going to hang onto the principle, regardless of how foolish it may sound. There is nothing wrong with it." The mental process Fermi went through is no different from the one faced by someone who believes in the law of chastity, or the principle of the Word of Wisdom, or any other gospel principle. We should not ever be intellectually embarrassed about putting our faith in principles.

3. One thing we have learned in the space program, if we have learned anything, is that it isn't a good idea to make critical decisions under the pressure of an emergency. We need, as much as possible, to think about all our decisions very calmly ahead of time. We have developed a very elaborate procedure of simulations where we not only train the crew for a nominal or perfect mission, but we also face all the emergencies we can possibly imagine that could come up. We have a huge set of books called *Mission Rules and Malfunction Procedures*, which describes all the things we are supposed to do for every conceivable problem during flight.

During the Skylab mission, when I was a back-up crew member, I spent three and a half years doing simulations, including 3200 hours in the simulator trainers, and during most of those hours, things were going wrong. I had to decide ahead of time what I would do when a problem arose; then, if a real emergency should come up, I would know how to solve it.

For example, there is a particular way in which the computer of the Saturn V booster can go haywire and not allow the booster to go into its pitch program. As a result, the booster would go straight up rather than into

Following his space voyage, Don Lind talks to young children at the Hansen Planetarium in Salt Lake City

orbit, and when it ran out of fuel, the spacecraft would tip over and come straight back down. The problem is, if you enter the atmosphere straight up, you go up to about 62 Gs. But the spacecraft would start coming apart at many fewer Gs than that—and at that point, astronauts start coming apart too. This is what we call a clearly defined emergency.

The first crew to simulate this malfunction problem was one of the Apollo teams. They decided that as soon as they got off the booster, they would fire the engine in the capsule. This would cause them to make a glancing blow into the earth's atmosphere to reduce the G forces—but it also would land them in the middle of Africa. The ground controllers in the control center for the simulation frantically tried to figure out what to do with the spacecraft. They decided to use the curved surface of the heat shield to steer the spacecraft so it would drop into Lake Chad in Africa; this would allow a water recovery, which is what the capsule was designed for. But just after they had completed the fireball phase of reentry, a point of no-return, someone rushed into the control room with an atlas and shouted, "Don't do it! The average depth of Lake Chad is only two feet!" If the experience had been for real rather than a practice simulation, the capsule would have been buried in the mud. The last transmission was, "After you hit, don't try to open the hatch. We will try to dig you out as fast as we can."

The point is, it is best to practice for those emergencies ahead of time, during a simulation when we can think about whether we are doing it right. We don't want to really kill ourselves by making the decision on the spur of the moment when we're in the actual emergency.

Have you ever looked at a black and foreboding thunderhead, with clouds boiling up to 50,000 or 60,000 feet, and wondered what it must be like inside one of those things? Driving in a thunderstorm can be exciting, but flying through one can be even more exciting. In my business I do a lot of high-altitude flying, to give me training for flying spacecraft. I get this experience by flying T-38s to meetings and training sessions all over the country. I often travel to my work at 45,000 feet, just under the speed of sound, and with that kind of flying schedule, I am bound to run into a thunderstorm sooner or later.

The interior of a thunderstorm is not a friendly place. The vertical wind velocities are so violent that the plane's altimeter winds and unwinds as fast as the needle will move. Part of this effect is due to pressure changes, but much of it is due to the aircraft being swept upwards and downwards for hundreds of feet, bouncing around the sky. The instrument panel shakes so much that I see the instrument needles only as vibrating blurs. I begin to breathe irregularly, perspire noticeably, and hold onto the control stick and throttles with unusually white knuckles.

A thunderstorm has the capability to rip wings off an airplane; aircraft wings are guaranteed to stay attached only to 7.3 G's. The ice that forms hail in such storms will form even faster on the inlet guide vanes of a J-85 engine. If chunks of this ice break off and are swept back through the compressor section, they will tear off the compressor blades. Since the compressor is spinning at 8300 rpm, the blades will be flung off with roughly the velocity of a rifle bullet—sufficient velocity to make holes in astronauts! Anything spinning that fast, if unbalanced, will vibrate itself to destruction in about four seconds and will remove the entire tail of the airplane, which makes the plane very hard to fly. Planes have crashed because of ice formed on jet engines during thunderstorms.

The lightning in the thunder cells is another worry. If it hits the aircraft, it may cause structural damage. It could also reverse the polarity on the fuel pumps, which would flame-out the engine. I have been struck by lightning just once, and although only minor damage resulted, it was quite a thrill. You tend to remember things like that. If the flight is at night, a lightning flash even a few miles away can temporarily blind a pilot. If he is flying just under the speed of sound and can't see for fifteen or twenty seconds, he can be in very serious trouble. He may find himself going straight down when he gets his eyesight back!

All things considered, the inside of a thunderstorm is not the place to be, so if there is danger of entering one of these situations, we take precautions ahead of time. These are called thunderstorm penetration procedures. They do not guarantee that we will come out the other side, but they at least increase our probability of coming out the other side instead of falling out the bottom. The first thing to do if we are threatened with a thunderstorm is to slow down to 280 knots; the wings have the best chance of staying on at that speed. Next, we tighten the shoulder straps and seat belt so that we won't be thrown out of reach of the control panel. We need to turn on the anti-ice heaters just as high as they will go to prevent the ice from forming in the engines. This has to be done ahead of time; otherwise the heaters will just melt loose the ice and send it straight back into the compressor. For the structural damage from lightning, there is little else to do but pray. If it is night, we can turn up the instrument lights as bright as they will go and then fly with one eye closed; then when a lightning flash wipes out the night adaptation of the open eye, we can switch eyes, hoping the first eye will recover before the next flash. It is important to remember that we have to take all these precautions *before* we get into the storm. Otherwise they won't do us any good.

Now, what does this have to do with people who aren't flying airplanes? If we ever get up on "passion flats" and are breathing a little irregularly and perspiring slightly, we are already in the thunderstorm. There are situations in our lives that remind me very much of these thunderstorms, when the pressure is on and we feel as anxious as if we were being bounced all over the sky. These are the situations in which extremely important things depend on how well we do. Once we come out of a thunderstorm going straight down, we seldom get a second chance. We have to be able to think clearly even though the pressure is on. When we start feeling that pressure is not the time to try to decide if we believe in the law of chastity. This is not the time to be making important value judgments like that. We should have made that decision a long time ago in the calm of a non-stress situation. We need to review our thunderstorm penetration procedures before we get there. We must not ever say, "Yes, but that is never going to happen to me." The devil loves to take that bait. We do run into "thunderstorms," temptations that we can't predict ahead of time, so before we get there, we need to think through what we are going to do.

The Lord put us here on the earth to make decisions, some of them in the face of considerable temptation and pressure. My flying experience suggests to me that when the decision is terribly important, we should consider the alternatives even before a crisis comes up. We must decide ahead of time what principles we really believe in, what kind of a person we really want to be. It helps if we review our thunderstorm penetration procedures before we get into the storm, then decide whom we will listen to for advice. The Lord loves us and wants to help us succeed. Though Neil Armstrong was desperately alone in making his decisions on the moon flight and was the only one with hands on the controls, yet he really had a tremendous support team behind him who were anxious to give encouragement, advice, and help. We too are at the helm of our lives, making decisions alone, but there is a caring support team to help us—family, friends, and Church leaders who sincerely hope we make it. Let's cheer each other on!

Chapter 13

Preparing for the Skylab Flights

I was selected in a pilot astronaut group, but even though I fly, I have always thought of myself as a scientist first. I have tried to keep research projects going in addition to my astronaut duties.

When it appeared that the first landing on the moon was going to be only to see if we could get up and back in safety, and there were no scientific experiments scheduled (except to pick up a few lunar rocks), I got busy. My assignment at that time was lunar operations; another astronaut and I were to work out the procedures and timelines of what would be done on the moon. We knew just how long and how difficult each task would be because we had worked in spacesuits to practice each one. A number of scientists had experiments they wanted done on the moon but were told they would have to be saved for later flights. However, I felt that at least a few simple-to-set-up experiments could be done by the astronauts without taking much of their time or overtaxing them. Finally we were able to assemble a few experiments and work out the procedures and timelines for them. ALSEP would be sent up on the first lunar flight after all.

One experiment, designed by Dr. Johannes Geiss of Switzerland, would be very simple for Neil Armstrong and Buzz Aldrin to deploy. All they had to do was poke a pole into the lunar soil so it would stand upright. The pole had a type of foil on it to catch particles from the solar wind as they streamed past. At the end of the lunar mission, the foil was to be brought back and the particles analyzed. I succeeded in getting this experiment added to ALSEP; Dr. Geiss's solar wind experiment was taken to the moon on that first mission and on the subsequent flight too.

This was the beginning of a fruitful association for me. I have collaborated with Dr. Geiss and his colleagues on several space experiments. We even had the pleasure of having Dr. Geiss live in our home with us for several months prior to and during the first lunar landing. He is a most interesting man.

NASA had contracted to have twenty Apollo/Saturns built (I guess it's cheaper at bulk rate). Ten of these were to be used to prepare to go to the moon, and the other ten were for lunar-landing flights. After several landings had been made, NASA's budget was cut. Something had to be trimmed, so the last three moon-landing flights were cancelled.

There was sadness at our home because with this announcement, my chance to perform scientific experiments on the moon was lost. Here was the greatest scientific expedition mounted by man—the exploration of the moon—and it was conducted by eleven test pilots and only one scientist. I had fully expected to be the second scientist to go up. I kept thinking how silly it was to cancel the flights. To me, it was like having a big, beautiful, expensive Cadillac all paid for but leaving it parked in the garage because you aren't willing to pay the extra ten dollars for gas. The most expensive part of the project—the space vehicles—were already paid for and delivered, but now there wasn't enough money for "gas."

The very Saturn V rocket and Apollo capsule that could have taken me to the moon now sit parked on the grass at the Johnson Space Flight Center in Houston as a tourist attraction. I have to admit this was a disappointment I have had to learn to deal with. I sometimes still feel a pang as I drive by this rocket display that is simply rusting on the ground.

At about this time I was feeling not only disappointed but also discouraged, and I strongly considered leaving NASA. I had been fasting and praying and counseling with my wife on what to do. One day as I was flying home from a Church speaking engagement, praying for help in making a decision, the Spirit spoke to my mind. I was told, clearly and distinctly, that the Lord had helped me to become an astronaut, and part of the reason was so I could speak to and influence the youth of the Church. I might tell them the very same things their parents were saying, but because of the position I held, they might tend to listen to me instead of their folks. Some might even say, "Hey, maybe Dad was right. Brother Lind says it too!" The Spirit told me that I was being called on a mission to speak at youth conferences. The duration of this mission was even mentioned—two and one-half years. After that, the Lord would give me other assignments, but for this time I was to serve the Lord in this manner.

A peaceful feeling filled me as I accepted this "call." I had been giving talks frequently, but immediately I started getting many more invitations to speak. I could have given a talk almost every weekend, but I decided that the Lord would not forgive me if I saved the world but if, in doing so, I lost my own children by always being away. I got a big calendar that showed the entire year on one page. When I had filled in two weekends in a month for speaking assignments, I would leave the remaining weekends free to be with my family. I must admit that this didn't always work, and a few times I even spoke every weekend within a month.

When the two and one-half years were up, the invitations immediately dropped off, and only occasionally would I travel somewhere to speak. At that time I was given new NASA assignments that tied up my time, so it would have been harder to go off on weekends as I had previously been doing. There was no doubt in my mind that the Lord was in charge. When he gave me this mission call, I had more freedom from NASA than usual, but when the specific mission period was up, I received new time-consuming astronaut assignments.

NASA decided that the two remaining Saturn V rockets should each be made into a small, compact space station called Skylab. Three separate crews made up of three astronauts each were sent up in succession to man the first Skylab. I was on the back-up crew for the last two of these teams. I was also on the Skylab rescue team that would have gone up to rescue the men had they needed it. Actually, for a time we thought this would be needed.

When the second crew went to man the Skylab, they experienced the loss of some altitude-control thrusters on the service module of the spacecraft that would bring them back to earth at the end of the mission. We had planned for such a problem by preparing a spacecraft fitted with five couches and flown by two crewmen instead of the normal three. That left three empty couches in which we could bring back the stranded crew members.

Vance Brand and I had trained as the rescue crew. But we were also on the back-up crew, so while the launch vehicle was being prepared at the Cape for our rescue mission, it was our responsibility to get into the simulators to try to work out some emergency procedures so that the crew could return safely, despite the failed thrusters. Thanks largely to Vance's ability, we were able to figure out a way to do this, so just before the rescue mission was to launch, it was cancelled. I said to Vance, "Do you realize what we have done? We have

Don Lind conducts experiments in Spacelab trainer

worked ourselves out of a space flight. We should be given an A for effort and an F for stupidity." There went another chance to fly.

Before Skylab, the longest space flight had been fourteen days in length. The astronauts had tolerated this quite well, so the medical people felt that this number could be safely doubled to twenty-eight days for Skylab. Then if the first Skylab crew showed no ill effects from twenty-eight days, the second crew would stay fifty-six days. The third crew would also be up for fifty-six days because of the limitation of consumables: electrical power, water, food, and oxygen.

At the end of the second stay, things had gone so well that it was decided that the last crew could safely stay up longer. This crew ended up staying eighty-four days. The equipment and supplies needed for all three crews had been stowed on board the Skylab before it was launched, so when NASA decided to have the third crew stay longer, more supplies were needed. When the third crew was launched, they took with them a few extra supplies, including food (for one thing, they were out of catsup!). To make the clothes allotment extend out, the crew just wore the clothes a little longer before depositing them in the disposal tank. They didn't figure right, however, and began running out of underclothing about a week early. They radioed down to Mission Control and asked what they should do about the situation. The next morning came this message: "We have some good news, and we have some bad news. First the good news: We have found an answer to the underwear problem. Now the bad news. The solution is that you trade. Al, give yours to Owen; Owen, give yours to Jack; and Jack, give yours to Al." This got a laugh, but the astronauts didn't think the idea was the greatest.

The training was difficult but very interesting. In the two years I prepared for the Skylab flights, I spent 3200 hours in the training simulators learning how to handle every malfunction imaginable. But through all this there was also an element of frustration, since I knew I would not fly unless one of my friends became ill.

I was the back-up crewman for two of the most disgustingly healthy men who have ever lived. A back-up crew trains right with the prime crew; their training is identical, so that if a prime-crew member gets sick or breaks a leg or something, a back-up crew member is all trained and prepared to go into space in his stead. This happened only once, when Ken Mattingly was pulled off the Apollo 13 flight because he had been exposed to the measles. Jack Swigert went in his place on that ill-fated trip.

When I was back-up to Jack Lousma, he said, "Don, you have to make me a promise. No pushing on the stairs and no praying." I would have given my eye-teeth to go up to Skylab, but I would never wish anyone as nice as Jack anything but good. He came to me shortly before his launch and said, "Don, since you can't go up,

I'd like to do something for you. I would be glad to take something in my PPK [personal preference kit, which each astronaut on the flight can take] for you, so you will have something that has been in space." I thought this was most gracious of him. I sent two rings in his kit: my wedding band and a ring of Kathleen's containing a diamond for each of our children.

Twenty-one days before the launch date, each crew, including the back-up crews, went into quarantine. They were kept away from germs that might make them sick. Since the incubation for most illnesses is less than twenty-one days, NASA figured that anything they had been exposed to before going into quarantine would show up before the launch, so that if they were well at launch time, they likely wouldn't be carrying any new germs to make them sick on orbit.

During quarantine, both the prime and back-up crews lived in quarters at the Manned Space Center about a mile from home (so close and yet so far away). The housing was not bad, but it was lonely at night. During the day we went about our training activities. Kathleen could come to see me, but to make sure she didn't have anything I might catch, she had to have a doctor check her out before each visit. Then she had to wear a little blue surgical mask over her nose and mouth. The children were not permitted to visit, since they were considered "germ factories." I was in quarantine for both the second and third flights, and our children began to feel I had been kidnapped (or "daddy-napped"). They were threatening to make signs that read "Let our Daddy go!" and picketing the crew quarters (like Moses before Pharaoh saying, "Let my people go").

Our former bishop, Clayton Huber, was in charge of the food for the space flights at that time. In fact, he is one of the heroes of the space program, having taken the food the astronauts have to eat in orbit from foul-tasting paste squeezed from tubes (in the Gemini days) to the gourmet fare that the astronauts enjoyed in Skylab. All we could really say for the first food was that it was life sustaining. Dr. Huber's food was really very good, but the crews would always crave something they weren't getting. I remember a discussion that we had both times I was quarantined. They were different crews, but each said about the exact same thing: "Boy, when I get out of here, the first thing I want is a six-pack of beer." Then they turned to me and asked, "What do Mormons crave?" I replied, "I'm drooling for a chocolate milk-shake!"

They were running a total body-chemistry test on the Skylab flights. This meant that every day, even in quarantine, we consumed the same amount of nutrients. If we didn't eat all our mashed potatoes, we had to swallow enough nutrient pills to make up for what we didn't eat; it really was easier to just eat it all and not have the hassle of the pills. Bishop Huber and Kathleen would come to my quarters and have sacrament meeting with me. These were beautiful, special times. Kathleen brought bread for the sacrament, but I had to save a piece of my daily allowance of bread in order to partake. I have never been in a sacrament meeting with fewer people, but we felt the Spirit and knew that the Lord was speaking also of our gathering when he said, "When two or three are gathered together in my name, there am I in the midst of them." (Matthew 18:20.)

NASA again suffered budget cuts, and with them, cancellation of the second Skylab. This 85-ton manned laboratory was cut apart and put on permanent exhibit at the Smithsonian Air and Space Museum in Washington, D.C. I felt almost as though I was being cut up when they did that. The procedure had been for the back-up crew to be the next prime crew that would go into space. Here again, *my* flight was being cancelled. But somehow it didn't hurt quite so much this time, because I felt the

Lord had me in this position as an astronaut, and I would let him determine what I would do.

Earlier, when I realized that I wasn't going to the moon, it was a traumatic experience, and I had to reevaluate what was really important. I realized again what I knew all along—being an astronaut is not my most important calling. I remember a discussion Kathleen and I had in which I said that getting to the moon couldn't be all that important because probably fifteen years later only she and I would remember if I had made it there. Can anyone remember the names of all twelve men who went to the moon? But if one of my children was in the state penitentiary or had just gone through a horrible personal trauma, *that* would be important. What I do as a father is obviously more important than what I do as an astronaut. I came to the conclusion that only two things really count much—what we do for our family and what we do to build the Lord's kingdom. The rest of it is pretty trivial. Whether I walked on the moon just wasn't that important, and the world would go on if I didn't have a Skylab flight.

In addition to my back-up crew activities, I was the principal investigator, or chief scientist, for one of the many scientific experiments aboard Skylab. In my experiment, called "The Magnetospheric Particle Composition Experiment," particles that came from space and from the Northern Lights were trapped.

When the last astronauts returned to earth bringing back the collection from my experiment, Kathleen and I went to Europe for ten weeks so I could begin to analyze the experiment data. This was done at the University of Bern in Switzerland in collaboration with Dr. Geiss. We lived near the Swiss Temple, and while I worked at the university, Kathleen was able to spend many happy hours there. We were both thrilled by the inspired and enlightening sacred lectures given there by Emil Luschin, the temple president.

My parents came to Houston to stay with our children, making it possible for us both to be away. Before we left, our bishop, Garth Ladle, told us he felt inspired to say we were going on a type of mission for the Lord. He said that what we would do to build the kingdom while on this trip was more important than anything else we could do in Europe. How prophetic this was! We didn't think anyone in the Church knew we were coming, but somehow they did. The branch president from Zollikofen met us at the airport in Zurich and told us he felt the Lord had sent us, so he was going to put us to work. In the ten weeks we were there, we were to speak forty times for the Church in sixteen different cities and seven countries, with audiences ranging from 50 to 1000. This is not counting the talks given for NASA, the university, and the United States embassies.

In a trip that was filled with many high points, one of the most memorable experiences was our week in the Holy Land. We were blessed to have personal guided tours by three wonderful Latter-day Saints—David Galbraith, John Tvedtnes, and Ken Crook. I will never forget my feelings as I had the humble privilege of breaking the bread and blessing the sacrament in a small Church gathering at the Garden Tomb. Not too long before, while standing in this same sacred place, President Harold B. Lee had said that this was the actual tomb where our beloved Savior had lain and then been resurrected. We sang a favorite hymn that goes: "There is a green hill far away without a city wall, / Where the dear Lord was crucified, who died to save us all." But at this place, we changed the first line and sang, "There is a green hill near at hand." We truly felt the Redeemer "near at hand."

We went to see the huge archaeological dig Tel Megiddo, where archaeologists have found evidence of twenty different cities, one on top of another. The oldest city dates clear back to King Solomon's time. We were very moved as we realized that this place and the valley beside it are also called Armageddon, which the scriptures tell us is to be the site of the last great battle before the Savior's second coming. All the time we were there, Israeli phantom jets were flying overhead on bombing runs on Mount Hermon near the far end of the Sea of Galilee. We were in a country that was at war at that moment, which gave us reason to pause and reflect on our own preparation for the final days.

All of these experiences were strengthening us for a trial that would soon arrive in our lives. On July 29, 1974, I was hit by a car while riding a bike. Kathleen needed the car for some errands that day, so I rode to work on our son David's bike. I stopped for a red light, then started across the street after the light turned green. My view was obstructed by a dirt pile from some construction, and a car ran the red light at about fifty miles per hour. The bumper hit my ankle, shattering it. I was thrown up on the hood, and my head caved in the safety glass of the windshield; luckily it didn't break through. Suddenly the driver threw on her brakes, causing the car to practically stand on end, and throwing me off. When both the car and I came to a halt, I was halfway under the hood and six inches from her wheel. If she had let up on the brake at this point, the wheel would have run over me. I was laid up for about four months with several broken bones.

One day while I was hospitalized, Astronaut Bill Lenoir, who had been on the Skylab back-up crew with me, came for a visit. Though it was a very hot summer, he was bundled up in a trench coat, looking a bit plump and secretive. He quickly shut the door to my room and pulled out from under his coat a delicious thick chocolate milkshake—the kind I had dreamed about while in quarantine with him. Actually, three different milkshakes were smuggled to me that day!

Chapter 14

The Goal Is in Sight

The fall of 1975 found our family in Fairbanks, Alaska. I had taken sabbatical leave from NASA for a year to do postdoctorate work at the University of Alaska's Geophysical Institute. I had several space experiments in the works on the magnetosphere and the aurora, so this was a great opportunity to go to the experts for training and to study the aurora firsthand.

It felt good to be back in school, although it was a dramatic change from the past three and a half years of Skylab flight simulations. Among other things, I was taking a class in plasma physics, which presented tremendously long and involved mathematical problems to solve. One day I came home moaning, "I have *three* problems to do by next Monday!" One of my children said, "Big deal! I have *forty* problems to do by tomorrow." The big deal was that just to write an answer to each of my problems took at least three entire pages of closely written data and pages and pages of calculations. But it proved to be a very fine experience.

At this time in the space program there were no space flights. The Space Shuttle was being developed, and it wouldn't be operational for about five years. Up to this time all spacecraft could be used only once. Now we were going to the next phase in development where we would have a reuseable spacecraft that could be used

151

again and again. In the interim, scientists in the astronaut corps were encouraged to take a little time to pursue their scientific interests.

We enjoyed a beautiful auto and ferry trip from Houston to Fairbanks. There we rented a nice home ten miles from the city on a beautiful wooded hill. In the fall we picked gallons of blueberries and wild cranberries. We watched in fascination as the days grew shorter, with less than two hours of sunlight a day by December as winter enveloped interior Alaska with a frigid blackness we had never experienced before. After the hot, humid climate of Houston, we also marveled when the temperature in Fairbanks reached 58 degrees below zero.

The year we spent in Alaska, Carol Ann was attending Snow College in Ephraim, Utah, and David was at BYU. They would soon go on missions, David to Sweden and Carol to the Maritime Provinces of Canada, the area in which both Kathleen and I had served. Our Alaskan adventure was so exciting for the rest of the family that we didn't want David and Carol to miss out on the fun, so when college let out in the spring, they flew up to Fairbanks to spend a month with us. They arrived just in time to attend an all-Alaska youth conference with Dawna and Doug. Dawna and I were on the conference committee, and Elder Paul H. Dunn and his wife Jeanne were our guest speakers. One of our activities was to climb to the top of a high hill to watch the midnight sun. Just as in the winter it is dark most of the time, so in the summer it is light both day and night. The youth have a saying in Alaska about keeping morally clean: "If it's warm enough, it's too light; if it's dark enough, it's too cold."

Dawna was worried about going to Alaska. She had had a goal for some time to be valedictorian of her high school class, and she was afraid that the change of schools would affect her grade-point average. But it didn't, and she achieved her goal the next year when we returned to Houston.

Doug did a lot of maturing that year. He was a great help when I had to saw and stack a huge woodpile just in case we had a power outage. Kim was twelve that year. She loved the scenery and had many friends in Alaska, but she wasn't sure she liked living in a "zoo without cages," after all the tales she heard about wolves and bears, and the moose and foxes we had seen running free. Each night she checked and rechecked to be sure all the windows and doors in our house were locked securely.

Lisa was five and started her first year of school there. Her school consisted of several house trailers. The Alaskan pipeline was being built, and it went right through the school grounds. During the winter the children had to go to school and come home in the dark, using flashlights to help them find their way to the bus stop half a block down the hill.

After my parents' children were grown and on their own, Mother and Father went on a mission to Australia. They spent a year there and then were called to finish their mission as temple workers in New Zealand. While there, Daddy became ill; he was never completely well again. He lived another six years, often in pain, but he never stopped and he never complained. He was a great example to me of patience and long suffering. He passed away while we were living in Alaska. Kathleen was pregnant at that time, and when I talked to Mother on the phone and she told me Dad had just left us, I thought, "Isn't it sad that he won't get to know his new grandchild who is coming." Then the knowledge immediately came to my mind, "He will know him before you do."

I went to Salt Lake City to the funeral, and before I could get back to Fairbanks, our seventh and last child, Daniel, was born, six weeks early. He weighed just three

The Lind family in Alaska, 1976: front, Kim, Don (holding baby Daniel), Kathleen, Lisa; back, Dawna, David, Douglas, and Carol

pounds six ounces, but he was so healthy that he didn't lose even an ounce. He received his name and blessing on July 4, 1976, the bicentennial birthday of our nation's independence. Kathleen had been ill through most of her pregnancy, but she will tell you he is worth all that she went through to get him here. It was wonderful to have another baby when the other children were somewhat older. We all appreciated and enjoyed him. We felt that the Lord had blessed us greatly.

When we returned to Houston, my new assignment with NASA was to help get payloads ready to fly on the Space Shuttle when it was finished. I was assigned to be NASA's liaison with the Canadians, who were making a huge articulating arm to go on the side of the Shuttle cargo bay. The arm would help deploy things from the cargo bay out into space, or to pick things up in space and bring them into the Shuttle. This work took me on a number of trips to Toronto.

At that time I had more experience than anyone else in NASA at the controls of the remote manipulator system (RMS), the fancy name we gave to the mechanical arm for the Shuttle. As a result, I was invited to a meeting in Los Angeles to discuss the design of the Syncom IV Communication Satellite System, which would deploy these satellites with the RMS (although by the time the first one was built, a different deployment scheme had been selected).

One of the officials at the meeting asked me how much clearance would be needed around the satellite to move it safely in and out of the cargo bay. I told him that if he would give us six inches, I could guarantee it could be done. If he gave us only one inch clearance, I could guarantee it couldn't be done. And if he allowed something between one and six inches, it would take me three months of testing before I could give him an answer. He turned to his senior engineer and said, "Let's see, the cargo bay is fifteen feet in diameter. If we leave six inches of clearance on each side, that will make Syncom IV fourteen feet in diameter." And as easily as that, I had just determined the diameter of a whole new generation of satellites.

In May 1983, Kathleen and I went on a speaking trip overseas for the United States Information Agency. We spent a week each in Germany, Bahrain, and Egypt. By then I was working on Spacelab 3 preparations. Germany was making the Spacelab, and it was particularly interesting to visit Germany's Space Agency, DFVLR, and climb in a model of Spacelab.

I worked for about a year developing payloads and experiments for the Spacelab 3 flight before the crew was selected. What a great day when the crew was announced, and I was on it! I would finally be going on my space flight. The crew would consist of seven men, with Bob Overmyer as the commander and Fred Gregory as pilot. There would be three mission special-

ists and two payload specialists—five scientists who
would be doing the experiments in the lab. I was designated as Mission Specialist no. 1; Dr. Norman Thagard
as Mission Specialist no. 2; and Dr. William Thornton as
Mission Specialist no. 3. The payload specialists, who
are not astronauts, would be Dr. Taylor Wang, an expert
in drop dynamics, and Dr. Lodewijke van den Berg,
whose work is in crystal growth. I think it is rather
impressive that four scientists—Dr. Wang, Dr. van den
Berg, Bill Thornton, and I—would be doing our own
personal experiments (in addition to the many other experiments) while on board the Shuttle together.

Spacelab is an impressive, very sophisticated, multi-
use laboratory. According to an official statement from
NASA, "The Shuttle is scheduled to carry a complete scientific laboratory into orbit. Spacelab is similar to earth-
bound laboratories but is adapted to operate in zero
gravity (weightlessness). It provides a shirt-sleeve environment suitable for working, eating, and sleeping
without the encumbrance of special clothing or
spacesuits."

As soon as the crew was announced February 11,
1982, we started our training in earnest. We held numerous sessions in the Shuttle and Spacelab simulators.
Each of us was given individual assignments to take care
of. Norm Thagard and Bill Thornton were to work with
the white rats and squirrel monkeys that would be on
board with us. No tests were to be done on them; we
wanted only to see how their automated cages would
work and how compatible to space the animals would
be. There was considerable concern when NASA discovered that essentially every monkey in the United
States had a form of herpes. Scientists had assumed that
human beings could not be infected with this form of
herpes; however, when NASA pressed for evidence on
the subject, the evidence showed that there was a real

possibility that men were susceptible to this form of the disease. Then there was a scramble to try to find disease-free monkeys to fly with us on Spacelab 3. Only two monkeys were found that were both disease free and felt comfortable in the Spacelab primate cages. These two little fellows turned out to be delightful traveling companions, and by the end of the mission they enjoyed watching us as much as we enjoyed watching them. When some of the debris from the animal cages got free while we were on orbit and floated about the spaceship, we were grateful NASA had insisted on finding disease-free animals for us to live with.

The launch date for Spacelab 3 was originally set for September 1984; then it was moved to November 22. We were not unhappy about this, since it would come just before Thanksgiving and our children would be out of school for a few days. Kathleen and I planned to take them all to Florida to see the launch. We felt they had earned a front-row seat, after all the years of love and encouragement they had given me.

Then the flight just before ours came back with a large number of thermal tiles missing from the Shuttle. Before it could fly again, the tiles had to be replaced, which would take several months. There was also a Department of Defense flight that needed to go up; this would take precedence and use our scheduled Shuttle and time slot. Our flight was subsequently moved to January 1985 and finally to early April.

When there is a delay in one flight, the schedule for other flights changes also, a sort of domino effect. When I came home and told Kathleen of yet another change in launch dates, she almost burst into tears of frustration. Many people needed to be contacted, and plans and reservations had to be changed each time the schedule shifted. I put my arms around her and said, "Honey, don't get upset. After waiting this long for a flight, what is another three or four months? Let's just go with the tide and enjoy the excitement of all that is happening." So that is what we did.

Though we had extra time to train because of the several schedule changes, we found the last three months before launch extremely busy. We were out of town at least three-fourths of the time, doing things that could not have been done earlier. I spent most of my time at Kennedy Space Center in Florida performing tests on flight hardware; doing simulations at Huntsville, Alabama; and at Santa Barbara, California, learning to run the experiments I would be doing in space. In an experiment that I developed, I would be taking pictures of the Aurora Australis. This was an extension of the work I did while in Alaska. For this experiment I was collaborating with Dr. Thomas Hallinan, a colleague of mine from the Geophysical Institute at the University of Alaska and an expert on the aurora and magnetosphere. Bob Overmyer would be helping me take the auroral observation pictures, so we went to Fairbanks at the end of January. Immediately after returning from this trip, I went with several other members of our crew to Marseilles, France (this was our second trip there) to learn to use the ultraviolet telescopic camera the French were making. This was to photograph dim galactic structures.

One day Don Reeves, patriarch of our stake, called and said, "I think you need to get away from it all and think other thoughts for a while. Let's take our wives and go up to the temple in Dallas for the weekend." I agreed that this was a great idea, exactly what we needed. Little did I know that this set the planning mills in motion. When we went into the final session of the day in the temple, we began to notice friends and loved ones there—our two married children, David and Dawna, and their companions, as well as numerous friends from our ward. Unbeknown to us, they had all come to spend this special sacred time with us.

After the session we had a testimony meeting in the chapel. Then we went across the patio to the annex building, where the brethren gave me a priesthood blessing. I was told that the launch would take place on April 29, the time it was then scheduled for. (From then on, we didn't doubt that it would go on the 29th. NASA wasn't sure, but we were.) I was told that the heavens were aware of what was happening in my life, that I would go and come back in safety, and that beings from the other side would assist.

What a blessed, sacred experience this was! It renewed our spirits. We knew that our Heavenly Father would bless us, and that all would go well with the flight. Just four weeks later our family and friends gathered with us at the Cape for the most exciting day of our lives. At last I was going into space!

"Go and Come in Safety"

Final preparations for our launch started about a week before lift-off. At L-7 (launch day minus 7) we began the health stabilization quarantine. We were cut off from association with everyone who might give us a cold or the flu. This meant that the only people who could be within six feet of us were those who had been designated "primary contacts." A person who was a primary contact had to have a special physical examination and to promise to report any sniffles. This group included all of our trainers and the simulator operators. If we had to move into parts of a building that were not manned by primary contacts, a security guard cleared the way for us and kept people at least six feet away.

Our wives were all cleared as primary contacts, but our younger children were not. The assumption was that since the children went daily to the largest germ culture in the city, the public school system, they were by definition carriers of an upper respiratory infection or something else equally unpleasant. Those of us who had school-age children living at home had to move into some special house trailers at the Johnson Space Center. These were located inside a hangerlike building where the light could be controlled, since half of the crew also had to shift their circadian rhythm. By steps of a few hours per day, they changed their sleep cycles so that

NASA

Don Lind poses with a model of the Space Shuttle at the visitors' center, Johnson Space Center

by launch day, half of the crew were day people and half were night people. That way we were prepared for round-the-clock operations when we got on orbit.

We kept enough of our work cycle overlapping while we were living in the trailers so that we could have a four-hour simulation in the Shuttle training simulators each day. The crew and the ground controllers practiced launches and reentries with complicated malfunctions intentionally planned to hone our abilities to a fine edge. We also had one meal with the whole crew together each day, and our wives could join us. We ate very well. The cooks who prepared our meals catered to our every whim, and everyone gained weight that last week. I felt like little Hansel being fattened for the oven.

At L-3 after the last simulation, we climbed into our T-38s and flew to the Cape. We made a formation fly-over of *Challenger* out on the launch pad and landed on

the special Shuttle landing strip. Our wives were there
to meet us; NASA had flown them in just fifteen minutes
ahead of us. The press and TV cameras were also there
to cover our arrival. We each said a few words at the
microphone and then were hustled off to the crew quarters, where we would stay until launch.

The last three days were filled with final briefings,
the last look at flight-data file procedures, and a physical
examination where our week of overeating was duly
documented. Time was also built into our schedule for
relaxation. Arrangements were even made for us to
meet our family members who were able to get primary-
contact badges for a picnic on the beach not far from the
launch pad.

Right up to lift-off, everything was scheduled to the
minute. We had practiced it all once before, even to
strapping ourselves in the Shuttle at the launch pad, so
the whole procedure felt very comfortable. We were told
not to set an alarm clock launch morning; we would be
awakened. If the launch count was running a few minutes late, our wake-up call would be shifted accordingly.
The exact length of our breakfast was in the master
timeline, as were hundreds of other activities, all march-
ing in step to the moment when the engines would light
off. It was like a great ballet, with hundreds of technicians and engineers and astronauts each dancing his
separate part, but everything was moving together so as
to have everyone and all the machines at the right place
and in the proper condition at the final chord—the igni-
tion of the engines.

At precisely the scheduled moment on April 29, we
were ready to leave the crew quarters, wave at our co-
workers in the hall, ride the elevator to the ground floor,
wave again at the TV cameras in the parking lot, and
climb in the special astrovan for the ride to the launch
pad.

By the time I climbed into the astrovan for that ride, I

had been personally involved in a significant portion of the manned space program. I had been selected as an astronaut during the Gemini program. I had helped prepare for the first landing on the moon, but my chance to walk on the moon had evaporated with the cancellation of the last three Apollo missions. I had trained as a back-up crew member for two Skylab missions and had been prepared for launch as a member of the Skylab rescue crew. I had completed specialized training in astrogeology, solar physics, orbital mechanics, and even medicine. And most important, I had had a front-row seat as a participant in one of the most important events of recent history. Now, as our seven-man crew rode toward the Shuttle *Challenger*, poised for flight at the launch pad, this was to be the end of my long preparation. I was finally going to fly!

I was surprised at how calm I felt as we strapped into our seats and systematically proceeded with launch preparations. But when the deep rumble of the main engines began, followed by the thunderclap of the solid rocket boosters lighting off, a feeling of euphoria swept over me. Part of it was little-boy excitement. Part of it was the realization that no managerial decision could delay us now. But a major part of it was the sheer ecstasy of high adventure.

For the first two minutes of the flight, we were surrounded by vibration and noise at a level that was impressive but not frightening. When the solid rocket boosters had completed their task and dropped back toward earth, the main engines seemed like an electric motor by comparison. Almost soundlessly, the force of acceleration grew to three times the gravity I was used to on earth. For a pilot, this was a familiar feeling. Then, after eight and a half minutes, the force suddenly stopped, and I floated up against the shoulder straps. A flight procedures book drifted slowly to the end of its tether and waved back and forth like sea grass in a slow

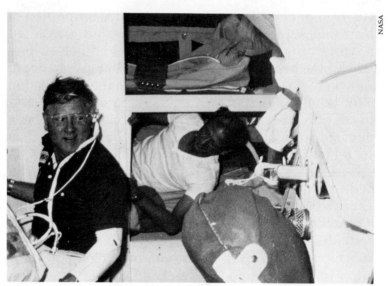

While Don Lind participates in autogenic feedback training, designed to help crew members overcome effects of zero-gravity adaptation, mission specialist Norman E. Thagard rests on the mid-deck

swell. This was zero-G. I was weightless. I was in space. I had finally made it!

For the first two days we were on orbit, I was extremely busy doing the tasks that justified my being there. Spacelab had to be activated, and the experiments for which I was responsible had to be set in motion. I hadn't had enough free time yet to really look at the earth. I had had glimpses out of the small window on mid-deck, and from a distance through the windows on the flight deck as I floated about doing my tasks. I had also been on the flight deck for several night passes across the Indian Ocean, dipping south of Australia almost to Antarctica to photograph and videorecord the aurora, the magnificent Southern Lights. But although the moonlit clouds sweeping past below me were truly impressive, nighttime was not the best time for sightseeing, and I always had to float quickly back to the

Spacelab to check on the growing crystals or change a film magazine or magnetic tape.

When I finally found a free moment on that third day, I was alone on the flight deck. No one blocked my view of any of the flight-deck windows. Our flight attitude was essentially standing on our tail, so I could see in one sweep from horizon to horizon and from directly below us to our zenith. There, 190 miles below me, was the great sphere of the earth, rolling past at 17,500 miles an hour.

Intellectually I knew exactly what I would see. I have probably looked at more pictures taken in space than most men, except for a few specialists. A visitor arriving from space would first see the earth as a planet covered with massive oceans and dappled almost everywhere with clouds. I know that the earth is large, but to see this huge blue and white ball wheeling majestically below me was overwhelming. From our altitude, the earth did not look like a huge flat map, as it does from even a high-flying aircraft. Instead, it curved away in all directions to the far horizon. There is no sharp edge to the horizon; the atmosphere gradually changes from the blue-gray haze of the horizon through a spectacular transition of brighter blues almost to white, then to deep gray, and finally to the velvet black nothing of empty space.

I have done some oil painting, and it would take twenty shades of blue to paint just the edge of the atmosphere, with another twenty shades of white tinged with peach and yellow and orange for the clouds. And I doubt that I could mix blues intense enough for the ocean depths. The shallow water of atolls and reefs and around islands sparkles in an unbelievable number of shades of green, blue-green, and yellow-tan.

The sight below me was so impressive that words or photographs are inadequate to record what I saw. Throughout my life I have been repeatedly impressed with the grandure of the Lord's earth, but never as intensely as at that moment. I was glad I was alone. Because of the sheer beauty spread below me, tears came to my eyes. (In weightlessness tears don't roll down your cheeks; rather they form extended watery globs in front of your eyeballs. Until they are wiped away, you have the wavering view of a fish trying to look out through the rippling surface of the aquarium.)

As I gazed down at the earth, many different thoughts crowded into my mind: the overwhelming beauty of it all, the millions of people who were within my view at any one moment, how close and yet how far I was from my loved ones. One thought that forced its way forward in my mind had been expressed by many of my astronaut friends as they returned from space—that mankind was so much alone in an immense, hostile void. I too felt that, but in a slightly different way. Both from revelation and from scientific analysis, I am convinced that there are many other peopled planets in the universe. I also accept as fact that there is a realm of spirit beings about us as real as the physical associates we work with daily. But even though I was intellectually aware of these other beings like us, when I looked down on planet earth, I had an extremely strong feeling that the people down there whom I loved were incredibly isolated on a beautiful but tiny blue and white planet in an unimaginably large void of empty blackness. In a mortal sense, this gave an entirely new intensity to the concept of the brotherhood and interdependence of man.

While looking at the full sunlit earth from outer space, we cannot see any stars at all; the sky is totally empty. With proper visual night adaption, the sky from space is, of course, filled with more stars than one can see from the darkest desert. But even without adapting my eyes, I could intellectually combine the earth scene below me with a view I had had of the heavens sometime before.

In that earlier experience, I had been flying a T-38 one dark moonless night, returning from a meeting on the West Coast. At 40,000 feet the night sky is absolutely clear, and with the cockpit lights dimmed, the sky was filled with more stars than someone on the ground ever sees. The sun had just set, and the zodiacal light—light from near the sun that is scattered by dust particles in the plane in which the planets move—stretched up from the horizon a quarter of the way across the sky. I had never seen it so bright. The zodiacal light and the planets that I could easily see defined clearly the ecliptic plane, that great imaginary plane in the sky upon which all the planets move in their journey around the sun. As I looked out from the T-38 that night, that imaginary plane was visually outlined across the sky, and intersecting it at a high angle was the plane of our galaxy, marked clearly by the myriad of stars of the Milky Way. Thus brightly sketched on the sky were two great astronomical pinwheels: the spinning galaxy of the stars and the spinning solar system of the planets. I could see in one sweeping glance a reality I had not gleaned from a dozen astronomy texts up to that time.

Now, as I looked out the windows of *Challenger*, I combined that remembered picture of the sky with the present scene of the earth below me and had a picture of the majesty of the Lord's creation more compelling and spectacular than I had ever had before in my life. Fragments of scriptures about how the glories of God's creations testify of him ran through my mind. "The heavens declare the glory of God; and the firmament sheweth his handywork." (Psalm 19:1.) This moment alone, gazing down at the earth and with all the emotions and feelings that came with the view, will always be one of the highlights of my flight on the Spacelab 3 mission.

Another scene that will always characterize this mission for me is the view we had of the aurora, the south-

"Group portrait" of seven astronauts in cargo bay of earth-orbiting Space Shuttle Challenger

ern mirror image of what I had always called the Northern Lights. I had devised and was conducting an experiment to record this spectacle of nature in a way that had never been done before. Our orbital motion swept us past the aurora so fast that with a high-sensitivity TV camera, we could record and later reconstruct the three-dimensional rapidly changing aurora structure. Pictures taken a fraction of a second apart from the stream of TV frames form stereo pairs to record this three-dimensional information. The camera recorded flickering and pulsating changes of the aurora that had been missed by the slower photometeric systems flown in space before this. A TV camera on the ground could record only a small circle of the pole-girdling aurora, but we could sweep past and record a major portion of the auroral oval before the magnetic conditions had time to change.

Studying the aurora was part of the space research program I had been involved in for years. I thought I was well acquainted with the aurora. I understood how electrons streaming down from space smash into the earth's upper atmosphere, causing the atoms and molecules to glow in pure colors of light, and I wanted to try to understand what mechanism fired those electrons from the magnetic tail of the earth down into the atmosphere. Scientists have some ideas about this, but no one is really sure of the whole process. The changing patterns that the electrons paint on the atmosphere—two giant undulating circles, one around each geomagnetic pole (one at the North Pole and the other at the South Pole)—tell us about the magnetic field surrounding the earth. This magnetic field, the magnetosphere, interacts with particles from the sun, causing magnetic storms that wipe out long-distance radio communications and cause power surges on electrical power lines. This is part of our environment that we are trying to understand and perhaps control.

I have seen dozens and dozens of aurora, but to see them from space is quite another thing. Individual sections of the aurora frequently form arcs hundreds of miles long that look like enormous shimmering draperies. These appear as bluish-green curtains of fire rising from the upper atmosphere toward us. These ever-changing curtains are occasionally capped with Chinese-red mantles and are frequently bordered at the bottom with delicate pink. To see these light forms shimmering and weaving below me from horizon to horizon was breathtaking.

In addition, I was aware that the electrical current circulating in the aurora was approximately equal to the power being carried by the entire North American power grid—Bonneville Dam, Hoover Dam, and all the rest added together. I was awed by the tremendous power as well as the spectacular beauty of the scene. I must admit that although I understood the physics of what I saw and can tell you the atomic or molecular transitions that make each shade of light, all that was only in a back corner of my mind. I knew which plasma instability caused the aurora curtain to continually curl, unwind, and reform. But I must admit that to see the whole world below me flaming and dancing with this spectacular light show of blue-green fire was much more beauty than science.

The week on orbit was a steady schedule of experimental work and procedural operations. Time on orbit was too valuable to waste even a minute. I have seldom worked harder than I worked that week. Learning to live in weightlessness was a whole new experience. Sleeping was no problem. Meal preparation was different but easily managed. The infamous toilet provided the counterpoint that makes the pleasant experiences all the sweeter. The Peter Pan ability to float to any corner of the laboratory and perch on any protrusion was the stuff night-dreams are made of. And the return of gravity during reentry was positively distasteful after the week of fairylike freedom.

My memories of the flight of Spacelab 3 are not all excitement, work, and science. There are a few quiet, personal special memories that are very important to me.

Several times I thought of the beautiful blessing I had been given at the Dallas Temple the month before our flight. Every time things needed fixing on our flight, I wondered if my dear father was there helping us fix them. There was never a more able fix-it man. I'm sure that if he had had the chance, that is where he would want to be.

Kathleen told me of an experience she had during the night we went up. At about midnight, she got a phone call from Kit Overmyer, Commander Overmyer's wife, who was concerned because she wasn't getting much information about what was going on up on the Shuttle (the radios she and Kathleen had been given so they could listen to air-to-ground transmissions were not working). On TV she had heard a newscaster report that the water in our galley wouldn't turn on. If we didn't get purified water, we would have to terminate the flight and come down without completing our mission.

Kathleen and the family had just returned to the motel where they were staying, after a lovely reception the Cocoa Stake had given for our family and friends who had come for the launch, so this was the first she had heard of the problem. She turned on the TV and heard words like "The astronauts will soon be in extremes for water." She called the family together for family prayer in our behalf. The next morning when she turned on the television, the commentator was saying, "The water problem onboard Shuttle has been miraculously cured overnight." She again called the family together to offer a prayer of thanks. At this time, the Lord spoke peace to both me and my family, reminding us of the blessing that I would "both go and come in safety."

Since our flight lasted a full week, we were in orbit on the Sabbath. The experiments went on around-the-clock and did not observe a day of rest. Nevertheless, I was able to shift the schedule enough to have a short time for my own private sacrament meeting on Sunday, May 5. My bishop, Melvin DeSpain, had given me permission to hold a sacrament service on the last Sunday before lift-off when I was in quarantine as well as the Sunday that I would be on orbit.

The orbital sacrament service presented some problems. The first was the sacrament prayers. I had taken a complete set of the standard works aboard *Challenger* with me. They had been sent to me by the *Church News* and the First Presidency, and were to be presented to the Museum of Church History and Art. However, they were stored where they were not accessible, so I could not use them for the sacrament prayers. Since we are counseled not to recite the prayers from memory, I had to find some way to include a copy of the prayers in the

official Flight Data File—the library of procedures we
have on board. That was really rather easy. One Flight
Data File volume is my personal reference notebook, so I
copied the prayers into the section used for diagrams of
auroral forms and communication procedures arranged
at the last minute.

The second technical problem concerning the sacrament was how to follow the scriptural direction, "After
this manner shall he administer it—he shall kneel."
(D&C 20:76.) In weightlessness, kneeling is not easily
accomplished. However, I managed to solve that problem. For privacy, I had planned to hold my sacrament
meeting in my sleep station, a compartment much like a
spartan Pullman berth. By kneeling on what might be
thought of as the ceiling, and resting my shoulders
against my sleeping bag, I could maintain the standard
reverent "kneeling" position—if I didn't worry about up
and down. In a way, this orientation had a special meaning for me. I know that looking upward toward heaven
is only symbolic of looking toward our Father in heaven,
since I don't know where Kolob is located on the celestial
sphere. However, I was strangely taken by the thought
that never before had I been able to kneel to show reverence and at the same instant face heavenward toward
my Eternal Father.

The whole experience was extremely moving and
very spiritual, filled with that special closeness to the
Lord that I normally can feel only in the temples and a
few other very special places. I suspect that this will always be the most memorable and special sacrament service of my life.

Besides preparing for the sacrament, there was one
other special arrangement that I had to make for the
flight because I am a Mormon. That was to be able to
wear my temple garments while in orbit. Normally that
could not be done. All clothing from the skin out is fur-
nished and controlled by NASA. The discussions for me
to be able to do this had gone on for several years. About

Scriptures taken by Don Lind into space are presented to Church leaders for display in the Church Museum in Salt Lake City. From left, Wendell J. Ashton, former publisher of the Deseret News; *Don Lind; Elder Thomas S. Monson of the Council of the Twelve; and Elder Dean L. Larsen of the First Quorum of the Seventy*

Wally Kasteler / Deseret News

a year before the flight, my bosses finally agreed that I could act as my own purchasing agent and furnish to NASA some Church-approved garments. A special NASA part number would be assigned so the stowage and quality-control system could handle this deviation from normal procedures. President Gordon B. Hinckley of the First Presidency had approved the whole plan, and to my great satisfaction, I was able to wear my temple garments into space.

I am sure that the general image of a space flight is that of impressive machines and billowing flame and the precision of high technology. And this is not incorrect. But in my memory there will always be additional and quite different elements: morning and evening prayers high above the earth; the renewing of baptismal covenants in a strange orientation while traveling at 17,500 miles an hour as I partook of the sacrament; the assurance that untold numbers of friends were praying for my safety; and a thrilling new glimpse at the grandure of the Lord's earth.

We fired *Challenger*'s engines to return to earth just a few seconds before crossing the sunset edge of the earth's shadow. By the time the burn was completed, we were in deep darkness. The first conversation among the crew was the very businesslike verification that we were headed on a proper course back toward earth.

The first casual comment during our descent was from the mission commander, Bob Overmyer. He told me that there was one of the best auroras he had seen directly ahead. Bob had been working with me all week in making the auroral observations, and toward the end, he had jokingly said he didn't want to see even one more aurora. I thought he was joking again, since now I could not get to the TV camera to record any more data. But when I floated out of my seat to look out his window, there it was, one of the most dazzling displays we had seen all week. So we flew through the upper edges of the blue-green curtain of auroral fire and returned to earth and to our loved ones after one of the most fantastic experiences of my life.

As we descended deeper into the atmosphere, the aerodynamic forces gradually built up, pressing us ever more firmly into our seats. We felt heavier and heavier. Finally Bob said over the intercom, "Well, gentlemen, that's 1-G. You're going to feel like that for the rest of your life." It was not a pleasant feeling. It felt more like 4 or 5 G's that I had experienced as a pilot during aerobatics. It felt as if I weighed between 800 and 1,000 pounds. When I heard the words "for the rest of your life," the thought came to me that this was what I imagine it would be like to come out of anesthesia only to find that both of my legs had been amputated. I didn't want to feel like that for the rest of my life. My next thought was, "I wonder if it was this unpleasant for Moroni to come down to earth." I quickly decided that celestial

Doug Lind

*Back to earth once again,
Don Lind holds
granddaughter Amber Kuhn*

bodies probably don't experience these particular sensa-
tions.

When we landed, we moved slowly and clumsily as
though we had on heavy suits of armor that we could
hardly support. As Fred Gregory tried to climb out of his
seat, he looked at me and said, "I'm surprised that the
floor can hold me up." This feeling lasted for a couple of
hours, then slowly decreased.

There were, however, a few moments when the feeling returned. When we arrived back in Houston, a large
crowd had turned out to meet us. My eight-year-old son,
Daniel, ran out of the crowd to greet me, and I stooped
down to give him a hug. Then, as I tried to stand back
up, I was heavy again. Only with difficulty did I make it
back to an erect position without embarrassing myself in
front of all the photographers. And during the first night
back home, I awakened during the night. When I tried to

get off the waterbed, I felt as though I had the heavy suit of armor on again. I thought I would have to crawl across the bedroom floor. But the feeling lasted only a few minutes. By the next morning I felt almost normal. Living back on the surface of the earth didn't seem bad at all.

Over the next few days it began to feel proper for me to be an "earthling" again. My body felt the correct weight. I remembered that I was no longer able to float or leave an unneeded item temporarily suspended in the air. The horizon did not rock slightly if I turned my head too quickly, as it had done the first few hours I was back on earth.

The marvelous week that I had spent in space began to take its proper place in my memory bank. The experiences and impressions of that week would remain vivid, but they began to fit into the context of the rest of my life. As I thought about what an exciting experience this had been, I was impressed by what a long and stimulating road I had taken from playing Buck Rogers in an elm tree to riding into the sky the fiery chariot called *Challenger*.

The preparations had been worthwhile and interesting in and of themselves, for I had learned so much. And the climax of the space flight had been both professionally satisfying and a great adventure. But this all seemed to slip nicely into the flow of the challenging and exciting generation in which we live. The Spacelab 3 mission would always be a cherished highlight of my life, but I began to wonder what new experiences lay ahead. What a wonderful time in which to live!